Manipulation, Body Language, Dark Psychology

Learning Everything About Mind Control, Persuasion, How to Manage Your Emotions and Influence People. With Secret Techniques Against Deception, Brainwashing, Hypnosis and NLP

Michelle Coty joseph bartkowiak

© Copyright 2020 by Michelle Coty joseph bartkowiak

All right reserved.

The work contained herein has been produced with the intent to provide relevant knowledge and information on the topic on the topic described in the title for entertainment purposes only. While the author has gone to every extent to furnish up to date and true information, no claims can be made as to its accuracy or validity as the author has made no claims to be an expert on this topic. Notwithstanding, the reader is asked to do their own research and consult any subject matter experts they deem necessary to ensure the quality and accuracy of the material presented herein.

This statement is legally binding as deemed by the Committee of Publishers Association and the American Bar Association for the territory of the United States. Other jurisdictions may apply their own legal statutes. Any reproduction, transmission or copying of this material contained in this work without the express written consent of the copyright holder shall be deemed as a copyright violation as per the current legislation in force on the date of publishing and subsequent time thereafter. All additional works derived from this material may be claimed by the holder of this copyright.

The data, depictions, events, descriptions and all other information forthwith are considered to be true, fair and accurate unless the work is expressly described as a work of fiction. Regardless of the nature of this work, the Publisher is exempt from any responsibility of actions taken by the reader in conjunction with this work. The Publisher acknowledges that the reader acts of their own accord and releases the author and Publisher of any responsibility for the observance of tips, advice, counsel, strategies and techniques that may be offered in this volume.

TABLE OF CONTENTS

Introduction 1

Part 1 – Dark Psychology 3

Chapter 1: Can Human Beings Be Psychologically Manipulated to Commit Murders? 5

Chapter 2: A Brief Introduction to Psychological Behavior to Read People 8

    Be Open-Minded 8

    Appearance Matters 9

    Read Facial Expressions and Physical Movements 10

    Notice the Tone in Which They Speak 11

    Study Their Emotional Energy 11

Chapter 3: The Dark Personality Triad 14

    What Does the Dark Triad Mean? 16

    What are the Characteristic Traits of People Belonging to the Dark Triad? 17

    Tips to Deal With People Who Have These Dark Triad Traits 19

Chapter 4: Everything You Need to Know About Human Predatory Behaviors 22

    What Are Predatory Behaviors? 24

    How to Recognize Predatory Behaviors? 24

    Common Human Tendencies Used by Predators Against You 27

Part 2 – The Psychology of Persuasion 32

Chapter 1: Principle of Reciprocity and Consistency 34
- Rule of Reciprocation 34
- Principle of Consistency 38

Chapter 2: What is Social Proof? 43

Chapter 3: How to Identify a Manipulator? 50
- They Always Use the Victim Card 51
- They Use Subtle Threats 54
- They Question Your Sanity 55
- They Use Sarcasm to Devalue You 58
- They Are Control Freaks 59
- They Always Think About What Is Good For Them 61
- They Will Constantly Blame You For Everything 62
- Their Mood Changes Very Frequently 64
- They Keep Changing Their Expectations 65

Chapter 4: Ten Approaches Manipulators Use Emotional Intelligence as a Trap and How to Escape? 67
- They Use Fear 68
- They Will Try to Deceive You 69
- They Take Advantage of Their Victims When They Are Happy 70
- They Misuse Your Trust 73
- They Use Denial 75
- They Have a Lot of Queries 76

They Try to Get the Best Out of Home-Court Advantage 77
They Have a Habit of Speaking Fast 78
They Twist Every Story They Tell 80
They Give You Limited Time in Everything 81

Chapter 5: Myths of Hypnosis 83

Myth #1 – Hypnotism Can Be Done Only On People Who Are Mentally Weak 85
Myth #2 – People Who Can Hypnotize Others Have Special Powers 86
Myth #3 – When People Are Hypnotized, They Become Helpless 87
Myth #4 – Hypnosis is Similar to Sleep 88
Myth #5 – You Will Have to Do Embarrassing Things 89
Myth #6 – You Just Need One Session of Hypnosis to Get Cured 89
Myth #7 – It is Black Magic That Gave Rise to Hypnosis 90
Myth #8 – The Patient Becomes Dependent on the Hypnotist After the Session 91
Myth #9 – Hypnosis Can Help You Remember Memories That You Have Forgotten 92
Myth #10 – I Have Never Been Hypnotized 92

Chapter 6: How to Hypnotize a Person? 94

What Do You Mean By a Hypnotic Trance? 94
Induction 96
Give Hypnotic Suggestions 99
Guide the Person Out of the Trance 100

Chapter 7: How Does a Hypnotherapy Script Work? 103

- Induction Script 104
- Deepening Script 107
- Subject Script 109
- Termination Script 110
- Tips to Make the Best Out of the Hypnotherapy Scripts 111

Chapter 8: A Brief Introduction to Mind Control 114

- What is Mind Control? 115
- Mind control vs. Brainwashing 118
- How to Take Control of Your Own Mind 120
- Advantages of Mind Control 122

Chapter 9: Dark Games People Use to Manipulate You 124

- Ultimatum 125
- Playing Hard to Get 128
- Implied Breakup 129

Chapter 10: How to Make People Obey Your Commands Through Mind Control Techniques? 132

- Gaslighting 133
- Fear of Alienation 136
- Repetition 137
- Flattery 140
- Guilt-Tripping 141
- Sarcasm 143
- Diversion 144

Chapter 11: Warning Signs of Manipulation in Relationships 146

    Your Partner Makes You Feel as If It Is Always Your Fault 147

    Your Partner Always Over-Delivers 148

    Your Partner Forces His/Her Insecurities On You 149

    Your Partner Does Not Communicate Clearly 150

    They Do Not Like Your Independent Nature . 151

    They Make You Feel Responsible For Everything Including Their Own Emotions 152

    They Often Use Negative Humor in Conversations 152

Chapter 12: How to Avoid Being Manipulated? . 154

    Have Knowledge about Your Own Fundamental Human Rights 156

    Stay Distant 158

    Avoid Self-blame and Personalization 159

    Ask Them Probing Questions and Keep the Focus on Them 159

    Make Use of Time at Your Advantage 160

    Learn to Say "No" Firmly and Diplomatically 160

    Set the Consequence 161

    Safely Confront Bullies 161

Chapter 13: How to Analyze People? 162

    Analyzing People Effectively 163

    People You Do Know vs. People You Don't ... 164

    Techniques By Which You Can Analyze People 168

Chapter 14: Psychological Tricks to Examine Human Beings 174
    Look Into Their Eyes 176
    Find the Hot Buttons 179
    Keep an Eye on Nonverbal Communication ... 182
    See the Person in a Light They Want to be Seen 184
    Tell Them a Secret 186

Part 3 – Emotional Intelligence 187

Chapter 1: What is Emotional Intelligence? 189
    Examples of Emotional Intelligence 191
    Importance of Emotional Intelligence 192

Chapter 2: How to Increase Your Emotional Intelligence Skills? 195
    Relationship Management 196
    Social Awareness 199
    Self-Awareness 200
    Self-Management 204
    Self-Motivation 205
    Tips to Improve Your Emotional Intelligence Skills 205

Chapter 3: What is Speed Reading and How Can You Do It? 209
    When Should You Speed Read? 211
    Techniques For Speed Reading 213
    Tips to Read Faster 218

Chapter 4: 7 Body Language Examples and
What Do They Show?...................................221
    Smile..222
    Arms Crossed on Chest....................223
    Eyebrows.......................................224
    The Head.......................................225
    Lips & Eyes....................................227
    Neck..228
    Crossing the Legs............................228

Conclusion 229

Resources 231

Introduction

Congratulations on purchasing *Book Title*, and thank you for doing so.

The following chapters will discuss different components of both manipulation and dark psychology, and you will get a lot of practical advice in these domains. There are three parts to this book. The first part primarily deals with Dark Psychology; the second part is about the Psychology of Persuasion, and the third part is on Emotional Intelligence. Once you finish reading this book, I am quite sure that you will have greater insight into not only your own actions but also that of others. You will be easily able to recognize if someone in your circle is trying to manipulate you, and you will also be able to escape their manipulation by using the techniques mentioned in the book.

In addition to what I mentioned in the first paragraph, the book also deals with how you can read the body language of people and analyze thought processes. Your formal schooling is not going to prepare you for everything in the real world because people can be manipulative, and you have to steer clear of the tactics of persuasion used by them.

This book aims to make a positive difference in your life, and I hope you get the answers to all your questions.

There are plenty of books on this subject on the market; thanks again for choosing this one! Every effort was made to ensure it is full of as much useful information as possible, please enjoy it!

Part 1 – Dark Psychology

Before you start reading this book, it is of utmost importance that you learn the meaning of dark psychology. When human behavior is studied with reference to your interactions, actions, or thoughts, it is termed as psychology. But dark psychology is something different – it refers to the science of mind control and manipulation. It is also important that you learn what manipulation means. If you do not understand the term properly, then you might be confusing it with other forms of influence. I know that every one of you have your own idea of manipulation, but it is for the best that I explain it here once for better clarity.

If we are speaking in the broader sense, then manipulation is when a person is trying to change your way of thinking or perception of things and the means to do that is usually exploitative or abusive. This is exactly what separates manipulation from persuasion. I know that questions might have already started popping in your heads. So, let us tie all the loose ends in the upcoming chapters.

Chapter 1: Can Human Beings Be Psychologically Manipulated to Commit Murders?

When someone is trying to manipulate you psychologically, they are basically trying to change your perception through the use of underhanded, deceptive, or indirect tactics. You can even call these tactics devious and exploitative. In simpler terms, psychological manipulation is a type of the social influence. But you have to keep in mind that not all types of social influences are harmful. Some are good too – for example, if someone from your family or friend circle tries to make you understand that smoking is bad for your health and you should leave it, then they are trying to persuade you into leaving your bad habits behind – this is not toxic. Social influence can be categorized as manipulation after judging the motivations and context.

Now, let us talk about the actual topic of the chapter – can someone by manipulated to such an extent that they commit murder? Well, if you want a straightforward answer to your question, then it is a yes, but read on if you want to know more about it in detail.

When someone commits murder, they are acting on their violent impulses and channeling all their pent up emotions into that one single act. Feelings of anger and frustration are quite common in our daily lives, and we come face to face with these feelings whenever we have to do some kind of confrontation with family members, co-workers, or anyone. When the control mechanisms of a person are ignored or almost non-existent, that is when the problem arises, and the consequences are pretty disastrous.

But you have to be induced to quite a significant level of violence in order to come to a state where you want to commit murder. And this is not impossible. It has been noticed that manipulation or listening to violent rhetoric can completely change a person's perception of things.

Some people are indeed genetically more predisposed towards violence than others. But even then, your genes are not changed by your experiences, but they can definitely be influenced in their way of expression. Various reports have shown that when a child undergoes a trauma that is not treated, they become more prone to crimes. Everyone has their own neural architecture that they are born with, but that does not automatically set you up as a murderer. The trauma that you experience or the neglect and abuse that you have to withstand is often the reason behind people becoming violent.

Similarly, if a person is exposed to long-term manipulation, especially at the hands of their primary caretaker or someone very close to them, then they can be manipulated to commit murder. Let us take the example of terrorism – it is probably the most prominent example of manipulation where groups of people are formed by constant manipulation. Then these people become ready to kill others. In fact, there have also been cults over the course of the years where people are recruited, manipulated, and made to commit murders in the name of following orders. Of course, the person committing the murder does not see it as a crime. In fact, they think that they are showing devotion and love to their leader, who was actually the one to sanction the murder and manipulate the minds of all those people.

Chapter 2: A Brief Introduction to Psychological Behavior to Read People

Psychology can tell you a lot about people, and yes, reading others' minds is possible only if you know how. Once you acquire this unique ability to understand what other people are thinking, you will notice significant changes in your work, social, and personal life. We are going to discuss each aspect of this chapter in detail when you reach Part 3 of this book, but for now, I am going to give you an overview.

Be Open-Minded

Before you learn how different psychological behaviors are interpreted to read people, you have to teach yourself to become open-minded. Otherwise, it will be very easy for your past experiences and emotions to overwhelm you and influence your thoughts. Whenever you are approaching a situation or interaction, be very objective about it. Don't give in to the temptation of judging people because that will lead you to misread them.

Sometimes, people think that if they want to read others, they can do so with logic. But let me tell you something – logic won't suffice at every stage. If you're going to learn to read the non-verbal cues of a person, you have to step outside the boundaries of logic and take help from other forms of information as well. Also, learn how you can absorb information from different sources without distorting the information yourself.

Appearance Matters

When it comes to psychology, appearances have a lot of weightage in terms of understanding and reading others. So, if you are trying to read someone, notice what they are wearing. Does their clothing exude confidence, or are they more inclined towards giving comfort greater priority? If the person is wearing something of spiritual significance, like a pendant or a bracelet, then you can learn about their spiritual values.

There is another term that is widely used in this aspect of psychology – 'identity claims.' You will find that some people wear t-shirts with slogans written on them. These people are deliberately trying to make a statement, and that slogan can actually tell you a lot about the person wearing it.

Apart from the clothing, you should also keep an eye n the person's posture. A confident person usually tends to hold their head high. On the other hand, people with a low sense of self-esteem usually cower down.

Read Facial Expressions and Physical Movements

We are going to cover this topic in greater detail in the latter part of this book, but for now, I must tell you that whatever a person is feeling, you can see their emotions on their face. Some simple examples can be –

- You can predict that a person is overthinking or worried if their forehead is showing deep lines of frowning.
- Similarly, if the lips are pressed, or the person has a clenched jaw, then they are trying to suppress their anger.

One of the simplest ways in which you can notice these in a person is if you engage in small talk with them. You will not only be able to familiarize yourself with them but also learn things about them that will help you to read their mind. It will also help you analyze in what way the person is reacting when the situation is normal. Knowing someone's normal will help set a benchmark for you and immediately identify when things are different.

Notice the Tone in Which They Speak

The tone of speaking or word usage is fundamental when you are trying to read someone's mind. For example, if someone tells you 'This is my second raise in six months' – they are intentionally telling you that they had previously received a raise in the course of six months. Such a person can be deemed as boasting and also someone whose self-image is entirely based on what other people think of him/her. When you praise them for the raise, they will feel good about themselves.

Similarly, the tone in which someone is talking is also important. Ask yourself whether the person sounds snappy or soothing.

Study Their Emotional Energy

Several strategies will help you judge the emotional energy of a person. For starters, you have to sense their presence. Every person gives off a vibe. This vibe is not always in terms of any action or words. It is just the person's presence in the room that will give off emotional energy. Try to sense that energy and ask yourself whether it is a friendly vibe or something that automatically tells you to back off.

The second thing that you can do is to watch the eyes of people. Take your time and look at their eyes while you are conversing with them. What do you see? Are they sexy? Caring? Sad? Angry? You should also try to sense the emotional energy radiated by a person when you come in physical contact with them, for example, a hug or a handshake. Was the handshake confident or uncomfortable?

Sometimes you also have to learn to believe your intuition. If you keep overthinking, you might not get the answer to your question. Just ask yourself straightaway – does this person make you feel good, or do you have a gut feeling that this person is bad? Do they make you feel motivated, or do they drain all your energy away?

Now that you know the basics of reading someone's mind through psychological behaviors, you should also understand that you cannot make any assumptions. Assumptions will be your worst enemy when you are trying to read or decipher someone's thoughts. It will bring a lot of biases and make your opinion of the person wrong, leading to wrong inferences. Lastly, practice is what will make you perfect. Keep watching and analyzing people. Study their facial expressions, their postures, and so on, and try to understand their feelings without any verbal communication. When you learn the skill of reading people, you can relate to others on a whole new level, understand their struggles, and also understand their true motives.

Chapter 3: The Dark Personality Triad

Both psychologists and the regular public has been fascinated by the dark side of every human being since ages. In this chapter, we are going to discuss the dark personality triad, which is nothing but a triangle formed by three personality traits that are independent but are very closely related to each other. And the only thing that is common among these three traits is that there is a certain level of evil connotation to all of them. These personality traits, when present in a person, make it challenging to have a conversation with them or deal with them, in general. Things become disagreeable very quickly, and these people are usually very arrogant, volatile, and domineering.

Now, coming to the triad, the three constituents are as follows – psychopathy, narcissism, and Machiavellianism. The people who have these qualities often have a toxic personality, and having intimate relationships with them is not only complicated but also derogatory to the other partner. The personality profiles of these people are created when the three qualities of the Dark Personality Triad overlap.

Here is an example that might help you understand better –

A woman was once the subject of identity fraud. All her financial instruments like the credit card and her bank accounts were compromised in the process. She lived in an apartment where she had to pay monthly rent, and she lived with her boyfriend. Naturally, she was under a lot of stress as she was questioned regularly by the FBI, and this caused a tremendous amount of anxiety too. But even after all of this, the culprit couldn't be caught. But she thought that at least her fiancé was with her in all of this. He was very supportive of her. The fiancé also took the responsibility of paying monthly rent but from the money that the woman gave him. To cheer her up, he brought gifts from time to time. After a few days, the landlord of the apartment called the woman. He informed the woman about all the rents that she didn't pay. It was at that moment that she realized that the actual culprit in all of this was her own fiancé. He was taking the money for the rent but was spending on gifts. She was in complete denial because this was a case of extreme gaslighting. She couldn't believe the fact that it was her lover who was doing this to her.

What Does the Dark Triad Mean?

So, let us have a more in-depth look into the Dark Triad and what it means. It was in the year 2002 when this term came into existence, and it was coined by Williams and Paulhus. You already know about the three characteristics that constitute this triad, but in this section, we are going to go into the details.

It is said that anyone who has the traits belonging to the Dark Triad is basically showing subclinical symptoms. If we are to simplify this, it means that the person is not fully suffering from ASPD – Anti-Social Personality Disorder or NPD – Narcissistic Personality Disorder, but they are showing some symptoms.

You probably all have an idea of what narcissism means, but here is a simplified description of it – it is a state where the person has a feeling of grandiosity, superiority, or entitlement. The person simply thinks that they are superior to everyone around them, and they basically try to dominate everyone they meet. They are forever on the pursuit of ego gratification.

The major characteristic of Machiavellianism is the manipulatory attitude. People who have this trait are always focused on their personal gain in any circumstance whatsoever, and they always focus on their self-interest. They are also very duplicitous and calculating.

Lastly, if we are to explain psychopathy in simpler terms, then I would say that it is marked by a bold behavior where the person is anti-social and repulsive and shows a lot of callousness.

What are the Characteristic Traits of People Belonging to the Dark Triad?

I have already explained the three traits of the Dark Triad separately, but it is time that you understand the overall traits of a person who belongs to the Dark Triad.

- **Deception** – The first characteristic that can be easily spotted in these people is their deceptive nature. They do not have any amount of humility or honesty. They are greedy and are not sincere at all. When research was conducted on the three personalities individually, it was found that all the personalities tend to cheat on their partners or family members when they think they are not going to get caught. On the contrary, when the risk factors were considerably high, it was found that Machiavellians and psychopaths continue to cheat. They are in the habit of continuous lying. On the other hand, if we are talking about the narcissists, then instead of being dishonest intentionally, they are more prone to self-deception.

- **Callousness** – As you must have understood by now, people who belong to the Dark Triad, lack empathy. But to understand this concept better, research was conducted focusing specifically on affective empathy. Affective empathy simply means the power to respond to the emotions of others in an appropriate manner. The research concluded that the Dark Triad personalities lacked affective empathy as well. In fact, the results were quite creepy because these personalities actually felt good when they looked at people who are currently sad. Similarly, they automatically became negative whenever they saw someone is positive or happy in their life. If we are to explain a bit more in detail, then psychopaths were found to be happy whenever they saw someone was in fear. Similarly, both psychopaths and narcissists were found to be happy when they saw the expression of anger on people's faces.

- **Big Five Personality Test** – This test was mainly done surrounding the qualities of openness, conscientiousness, agreeableness, neuroticism, and extraversion (Lewis R. Goldberg, 1992). Now, I just want to clarify something here because most people tend to get it wrong. Charisma and agreeableness are not the same things. Agreeableness is more like compliance, straightforwardness, and trustworthiness. All of these qualities are of the utmost importance when you want to form strong relationships. Conscientiousness was something that was found to be lacking in both psychopaths and Machiavellians. The level of neuroticism was the least in the case of psychopaths, and so basically, that is how you conclude them to be the most sinister of all. When it came to extraversion, narcissists were the ones who excelled in this criterion, and that is quite predictable too.

Tips to Deal With People Who Have These Dark Triad Traits

If you think that someone in your life has the traits belonging to the Dark Triad, it can be really hectic dealing with them, and so, here are some tips for you. You have to understand that the process is not easy, but it is possible with patience and the willingness to address these negative behaviors.

- **Handle the Anger** – The first step will obviously be to manage their aggression because it is something that is very often seen in people belonging to the Dark Triad. If those situations are not controlled, they can easily defuse into something bigger. It is quite easy to spot when someone is angry, even if it means that they are showing signs of passive-aggressive behavior (ignoring you or sulking). You can talk to them or distance yourself from them for a while, or you can figure out where all of that rage is coming from.
- **Don't Let Them Bully You** – This is extremely important. It is not right or healthy if you have to withstand verbal or physical abuse. If you are in such a situation, you have to take a stand against it and take some action. Even if the abuse is indirect, for example, if the person is belittling you on a daily basis or criticizing you unnecessarily, you have to find a way to hold them accountable for their behavior.

- **Identify the Manipulators** – We will go into greater detail about identifying manipulators in the next part of the book. But for now, you should know that when someone's Machiavellianism traits take the upper hand, they become manipulators. They will always be finding some excuse or the other for their hurtful behavior and try to make you say yes for things that you don't want to do.
- **Learn New Skills** – Dealing with people with Dark Triad traits is no cakewalk, and so, you need special skills. It includes Emotional Intelligence, and you are going to learn about it in the latter part of this book. Once you acquire these skills, managing these people would become easier, and you can also spot any kind of unwanted behavior at once.

Chapter 4: Everything You Need to Know About Human Predatory Behaviors

If a gazelle comes in front of a hungry lion, it is going to chase the gazelle. The basic concept behind a predatory and its prey is that there is always one party that is benefitting at the expense of the other party involved. Such predator-prey relationships are used as a metaphor for several relationships in our society. Human behavior is complex, and you will often find people trying to benefit from the loss of others. There are people who exploit others because they are going to profit from it in one way or the other, and these people are known as the predators of society.

It is completely undeniable that exploitation and competition are two things that already exist in our society. But identifying these predators is not that easy. This is especially because the predators have spent years hiding their darker side. So, even though they are among us, we might not identify them as predators the moment we meet them. In the case of children, it becomes even more difficult for them to identify the predators. Children trust others easily, and they have a friendly attitude. If you think that predators are only those you do not know, then you are wrong. It can be anyone – it can be someone from your family, a friend, or even a colleague. In fact, statistics show that the chances of the predator being a known person is 90%. Moreover, it is usually seen that these predators are well-liked by society. They also have a great life on the outside. When they choose their victims, there is always a strategic plan behind it. They might come into your child's life through the church, school, or any sports practice they take part in.

What Are Predatory Behaviors?

Before I explain to you how you can identify predators, it is essential for you to understand what predatory behaviors mean. These behaviors can be of different types. If you are in a relationship with a person whose intentions for you are not safe and would hurt you, then this can be called as predatory behavior. In fact, such people can even take part in sexual assault against their partner. Predatory behaviors also include groping and rape. Sometimes, people engage in predatory behavior because their ultimate aim is personal gain through something like robbery.

You cannot simply point out the predator in a room full of people. Predators are just like you and me on the outside. They do not wear anything different that will point them out, and neither do they look different. But if the predator is someone that you are in a close relationship with, then there will be common signs that you might be able to notice. Some warning signs are quite obvious, while others are not.

How to Recognize Predatory Behaviors?

If you want to be aware of the predatory people around you, learning to identify them should be on the top of your priority list. So, in this section, I am going to discuss some of the possible warning signs that you will notice if you have a predatory person in your circle.

- **Having Particularly Strong Feelings Towards Specific People or Groups** – Let us say that you have started seeing someone recently, and within the first few dates, you noticed that they are expressing very strong feelings towards certain groups. It can be anyone like the Jews or even the LGBTQ community. Basically, they might have stringent opinions about anyone, and they will try to communicate that to you several times. In fact, when things take an extreme turn, they might even try to communicateto you, directly or indirectly, the violent acts they want to commit against these people. I am not saying that depending on this quality alone, you should conclude your partner is a human predator, but this is definitely one of the factors. Moreover, you have to ask yourself that is this kind of behavior something that you are comfortable with or not.
- **They Are Expert Liars** – There are only some occasional predators who either do not care about hiding their true feelings or are genuinely dumb. But most of them are

expert liars and conceal their true motives very well. So, if someone you know often talks about anecdotes that involve manipulating others to get something, then they are displaying characteristics of the Dark Triad. Moreover, these people can easily embellish stories in such a manner that no one can detect what is true and what is false. You would be able to say if their side of the story is true or false if you were present in that situation. I know that this is more like moral flexibility and not predatory behavior, but this is one of the characteristics that you will find in predatory humans.

- **They Portray Themselves As Flawless –** People with a predatory attitude usually have a grandiose attitude where they will keep dictating facts about their life that makes them seem flawless. In simpler words, predators (on the outside) have a very charming personality, and that is why people love them until and unless they find out the person's darker side. There is no substance in their personal relationships, even though you might find them to be socially appealing. So, at the heart level, no genuine bonding can be formed. In other words, you can call them 'too good to be true.' They create their image of social acceptability because that is how they come close to other people and gain their trust in the beginning.

Common Human Tendencies Used by Predators Against You

Robert Cialdini is a social psychologist, and he went through several research studies and examined them thoroughly on conformity and compliance. His main aim was to find the basic principles on which human predators depend to make others do what they want or persuade them. The conclusion at which he arrived said that human predators are well aware of the strings that can be strummed in order to persuade people.

Even though all of us use these principles at some point in time or the other, the critical thing to keep in mind is that you should follow the principles ethically. But if someone with not so great goals in life uses these principles, they have the power to exploit people, and that is exactly what human predators do. But if you are to shield yourself from the exploiting nature of human predators, you have to know about these principles yourself. So, let's have a look at them.

- **Authority** – When people talk with someone who is in charge or authority of something, we automatically tend to obey that person. We think of them as someone who has a lot of expertise in the matter, and so, we listen to whatever they have to say. But, in the case of predators, they know exactly what the person in front of them wants. And so, they often fabricate their image and credentials to appear as someone in charge of things. They also display a strong dose of confidence in their attitude. There is a tendency among people that whenever someone speaks faster than others, we conclude them to be confident, and so, if this human predator has this quality too, they can conceal their predatory nature in an even better way. People usually don't ask for proof from such people and believe whatever they are trying to say.
- **Liking** – Think about it – if you are comfortable with someone in your circle and you love talking to them, you also tend to say yes to most of their requests. This is because you feel safe in the company of those people, and so, this perceived similarity makes you say yes to them. That is why, hu-

man predators are in the habit of using common interests, compliments, and things like that to build a relationship with you and establish rapport. So, they will appear to be a nice person, and gradually, you will be saying yes to their requests.

- **Reciprocity** – Suppose someone comes to you and does you a favor, you automatically feel that the favor needs to be reciprocated. You feel like you have to give them back. But predators use this feeling of reciprocity to get what they want. They will help you out of the blue even when you didn't ask for it, and later on, you will feel obligated to help them out as well. Moreover, these gifts or favors that they do is what hides their actual motive or personality as a human predator.

- **Scarcity** – Whenever something is not available in abundance, human beings tend to think that they are automatically special. It also happens when something is available only for a limited period. In this context, human predators use this principle to offer others with items that are scarce and, thus, precious to the person. It keeps those people on the hook, and the predator continues to get what he/she wants.

- **Social Proof** – We are going to talk about social proof in detail in the second part of the book, but for now, let me give you a brief intro. What happens when you are confused and don't know what to do in a particular situation? You take the help of other people and so you ask them for their opinion, right? The process of decision-making becomes easier when maximum people rule towards one of the options. If you have any human predators in your life, they will often wait for such a dilemma to arise so that they can snatch the opportunity to influence your mind and guide you in a specific direction that they want.
- **Consistency and Commitment** – When people make their commitments known to the public, they feel the obligation to live up to those commitments, and so they abide by them no matter what. It is mainly because people want to make others aware of the fact that their values drive them. But predators will use this against you. Do you know how? They will initially get you to commit to something small but then leverage you into committing to a much larger one. As the stakes keep on increasing, the people tend to give in to the predator and do whatever they

are told. The dark side of the human predators is well concealed and hidden until and unless there comes the point where it is not possible to disengage for the predator.

In simpler terms, if you want to nip this form of manipulation in the bud, you have to be fully aware of your own vulnerabilities as well. The predators will always be on the lookout of triggers. You can be duped at any moment, even when you think you were the most careful one. It can be during a very small conversation or something deeper and meaningful. You have to be very careful because the predator will make every effort possible to appear as a genuine person in front of you. You need to proof from trusted people. If you let someone to come into your life and strum your strings just like that, you won't be able to shield yourself from the predator. Stay cautious at all times.

Part 2 – The Psychology of Persuasion

In this part of the book, we are going to discuss various topics related to persuasion and why you say yes to some people even when you don't want to do what they asked. Once you finish this book, you will find that your love has a different kind of driving force, and you will be noticing a lot of personal change that will bring you success. No matter what you do or who you are, you are going to benefit a lot from this chapter and also learn to defend yourself from the persuaders in your life.

Chapter 1: Principle of Reciprocity and Consistency

In this chapter, we are going to explore the two principles of psychology – reciprocity, and consistency. These were explained for the first time by Robert Cialdini in his famous book – *Influence: The Psychology of Persuasion*. Both of these are common tendencies seen in humans and read on if you want to know more about them.

Rule of Reciprocation

The basic idea behind the rule of reciprocation is that when people display helpful behavior, they must be rewarded. But here, you will understand how this rule is used by some people to persuade you, be it in a social setting or the corporate ladder.

When someone helps you with someone, you automatically feel that you need to return their favor, don't you? In fact, this has become a norm globally and is accepted by everyone across the globe. This is also why people have an expectation towards others to get something in return for their own helpful behavior. This rule is widely used in marketing, whereby customers are manipulated into buying things. Similarly, there are people in your surroundings who use this rule for their personal gains and manipulate you into doing something they want you to do. So, in order to return a favor that the person did, you agree to do something in the future. In fact, you feel compelled to do so.

Do you know why the rule of reciprocation is so effective? It is because people express power through it and gain the other person's compliance. Moreover, let us say that there is a request you have to make, but you know that the answer to that request is going to be a 'no.' In such a scenario, if you use the rule of reciprocation, you can get a 'yes' to any request you want because such people can be persuaded only when you create a feeling of indebtedness towards them. Let me give you a very simple example – we often feel obligated that we have to buy the other person's lunch when they buy us our lunch first.

When it comes to practicing persuasion and influence, the rule of reciprocation plays a very critical role, and yet, it is one of those factors that are not widely recognized. Whenever there is some form of interpersonal transaction involved, persuasion and influence are two things you need to master. It applies to both business transactions and personal relations. Whatever your intentions or goals are, they can be fulfilled better if you are adept with the rule of reciprocity.

But first, I think it is important that you understand the prime difference between influence and control. When we talk about control, it is more concerned about having authority or dominance over someone. But on the other hand, when we talk about influence, it is about the power you have over someone else that will make the other person change their behavior or perspective.

The rule of reciprocation can be applied to any kind of generosity performed by a person – it can be a kind deed or even a material object. No matter what culture we are talking about, almost everyone has this tendency in them to repay favors or gifts. The reciprocation can be expressed in different forms, which mainly involve kindness. In fact, Richard Leakey, who is a celebrated archaeologist, has described that this system of reciprocity is what has kept the human race going since ancient times. The network of obligation that was present since ages is what made humans share their skills and food.

If you think about how socialization has been portrayed in the different cultures around the world, you will quickly realize that it is all about giving back, sharing, and taking turns to return favors. Moreover, when people don't follow this norm, they are often ostracized, and so this, in turn, forced them to obey the societal rules of reciprocation. No one wants to be termed as a parasite, and so, because of this societal pressure, people are often ready to go to great lengths. It brings me to my next point – what happens when someone used the rule of reciprocation against you? You are already vulnerable because of the expectations placed on you by society, and so, if a manipulative person notices that, they can exploit you into doing something for them that you would haven't done otherwise. Thus, these people learn to take advantage of your free help in some way or the other. It applies in romantic relationships too. Sometimes, manipulative partners can make you feel that they are giving way more to the relationship than you and so you will feel obliged to do more for your partner not out of love but just because you don't want to be deemed as someone who doesn't know how to return favors.

That is why every person needs to learn how you can differentiate between things that you do out of obligation and things that you are doing willingly out of love. The path to gaining that sense of judgment is not easy. You will fail to make this distinction multiple times, and you will be naïve, but that is exactly what will prompt you to become wise. But even after several years of experience, there will be instances where you couldn't figure out the real intentions of a person. One piece of advice that I can give you is that the more mindful you are about your own thought processes and motivations, the more aware you will be of that of others as well.

Principle of Consistency

The next thing that we are going to discuss in this chapter is the principle of consistency. Self-image and its importance to humans play a big role in the principle of consistency. Let us say that you have publicly made a stand about something – it can be an action or even a decision. Once you have made that stand, backing off would mean that you are inconsistent with your promises, and this taints your self-image. That is why people face interpersonal pressure to get things done once they have committed to completing those things. It is also said that consistency is not inborn, and it is more adaptive in nature. The world is a complex place, and if you want to survive in it, there are some values that you need to learn, and consistency is one of them.

Out of all the characteristics of a person, consistency is considered to be very desirable. Consequently, if you are not showing a consistent behavior, you will often be ruled as someone who is hypocritical and indecisive. That is why there are so many people who do not even acknowledge their actual beliefs. They do it just because they do not want to seem like an inconsistent person to the world. But the direct result of such kind of behavior is that many a time, people show outcomes or behaviors that are undesirable because they overthink about staying consistent and in the process, forget about what all can go wrong with the behavior they are displaying.

I am going to give you an example to help you understand the concept in a better way. Thomas Moriarty was a psychologist who conducted an experiment in 1972 on the New York City beach. He took a portable radio and his beach towel and chose a spot to sit down, which was approximately 5 feet away from a person who was randomly chosen. He sat on the towel for a few minutes, and then, he walked down near the water. After 2-3 minutes, another researcher tried to steal the radio. Only 4 out of 20 people attempted to stop the second researcher from taking the radio. In the second scenario, the first researcher asked the person next to him to watch over his things. It showed a huge change in the results. In this case, 19 out of 20 people attempted to stop the second researcher.

So, here you see that when people are asked to do something, they make sure that they do it; otherwise, they will be deemed as inconsistent. People think that it makes them look bad in the eyes of others when they don't keep up to what they had promised. I am giving you some more examples to show how powerful the principle of consistency is.

One of the simplest examples is that of religion. Every one of us is born into some religion, and even though some people convert into other faiths, there are many who don't and follow the same religion even though they don't believe in it from their hearts. This is also an example where people don't want to be portrayed as someone who is inconsistent or irresponsible. Similarly, in the case of marriages, sometimes things don't work out as you had planned them to be. Does that mean you have to remain in this bond forever? No, because you also have the option of divorce. But there are many people who don't opt for divorce just because they have taken vows of 'till death do us part' and so, they won't go back on that promise. In that case, both people suffer. The feelings have died, but they are together only because of public commitment.

What people don't see is the internal conflict and pressure that goes on with the person just because they have committed to something publicly, and now, they cannot go back on their word. But if you look on the bright side, if someone is able to practice the principle of consistency in moderation and in a healthy way, then it can actually help you reach your goals.

The principle of consistency is not very difficult to understand. No one wants to break the principle of consistency because they don't want to seem unpleasant to other people. In fact, people try every method possible to align everything in the same line by either trying to rationalize things which they know is not right and change their self-perception in some way or the other. No one wants to be deemed as untrustworthy. When that happens, people stop giving you the attention, and you are pretty much alienated. In order to avoid that, people give in to the principle of consistency.

Moreover, if you think that outsiders are the only ones who judge you, then you are wrong. This is because all of us judge our own selves, and that judgment is usually harsher than anyone else's. No one knows your beliefs, intent, and thoughts better than you, and so when you start judging yourself, it is harsh. And if you find that your thoughts and your actions are not in one same line, you have to explain it to yourself – that is how things work. Now, it is human nature that no one wants to change their beliefs as such, so the first thing that everyone does is that they try to rationalize the situation by finding external reasons. But when we run out of points that can help us to justify our actions, we have to make some changes to our inner self.

The research that was done by Cialdini stated that when people are consistent with their decisions, they feel happier, but whenever there is inconsistency, they get confused and disappointed.

Both of these principles are easier said than done. If you want to master them, you need to be patient and consistent – quite paradoxical, isn't it?

Chapter 2: What is Social Proof?

By nature, all of us humans can be influenced very easily. It happens even more when we are in a setting that is unusual to us – we always look up to someone else who can help us out. Depending on the advice that we get, we act in a certain way, and if you think you were the only one who did this, then you are wrong because there is actually a scientific theory behind this known as the social proof theory.

Some people think that this happens only when you are new to some setting, but that's not it. It happens all the time, as you are going to see in this chapter.

Let us say you are fresh out of college, and you are still in unknown waters of the adult world trying to figure things out for yourself. You will find it in your heart that somehow or the other, you assume that everybody around you knows a bit more about things than you. It's like this magical manual that everybody got except for you, and so you are lagging behind in stuff. Everybody around you seems to be doing everything the way they should be done. They know how to make new friends, and they know what to do to get a dream job. But this is what you are thinking – the reality is quite different. Just like you, all those peers you see around you are at the same crossroad as you, and they are also doing the same things. But it is a human tendency to always look at others in order to find some path. That tendency never really goes away.

The moment we start feeling anxious or don't know what to do in any situation, we look for advice from people who can tell us what to do and what not to do. It is said that social proof exists or arises because it is in human nature to always behave in the right manner or try to fit in every situation they are in. I know that the easier way is to simply think that everyone else knows more than you, but you have to remind yourself that it is not the reality. It doesn't matter when you are in a private setting or a public; social proof can manifest itself in every place.

Now, I am going to show you how social proof can actually be troublesome or create problems. There are two good reasons for this. The first reason is that when people assume things, especially when present in groups, they can arrive at a conclusion that is completely meaningless, or worse – outright wrong. There is a special term that is used to describe such type of behavior in people, and it is known as herd behavior or groupthink behavior. In such a case, people might arrive at dangerous conclusions without even realizing it. The second reason is that people can manipulate you with the help of social proof and steer you in a direction that will support their personal motives. In these situations, people end up making choices that are so unlike them, and they wouldn't have otherwise made that choice.

When things take an extreme form, anti-social or violent behavior is encouraged because of social proof. When people are in the habit of pointing out your mistakes, you automatically become conscious of your actions, and you do not want to make any wrong decisions or commit mistakes. But the more this feeling of uncertainty, the more people give in to the idea of social proof. Another factor that acts as a fuel to the fire is when you find some form of common ground between you and those around you. This common ground can be anything – it can be your race, your class, your gender, or anything that is common between you and the other person. In such situations, people make it a habit to do whatever that other person is doing just because they share something in common. This is not just a habit but has a scientific basis to it and is linked to the neurons behaving in a specific way in your brain. This kind of behavior is termed as implicit egotism.

From the outside, we all think that we have the individual ability to do things, but somewhere or the other, there will come the point in everybody's life where we conform to the norms or opinions held by a majority of people. This is also popularly known as the bandwagon effect. The more people adopt an idea, concept, or trend, the greater number of people will be influenced to do the same thing.

A simple example from our day-to-day life should portray the concept of social proof even better. In the case of lawyers, you will often see them giving references from previous cases, but do you know why? The lawyer's counterpart will see how prevalent it is for similar cases to settle for a certain amount. Because of social proof, the counterpart can be persuaded to conform to a similar settlement offer as well.

In the previous chapter, I had already told you about Robert Cialdini. He had outlined a total of six principles of persuasion, and social proof is one of those six principles. If you want to persuade people, social proof will act as an effective tool when used in combination with consistency, reciprocity, scarcity, liking, and authority.

A few researchers had conducted a study on social proof. These researchers were from the New York

City university. A man that was selected by them was asked to stand on a busy sidewalk, and then he was asked to halt for a few minutes and look in the upward direction (Stanley Milgram, 1969). The researchers behind this experiment were Berkowitz, Bickman, and Milgram. The main aim of this experiment was to see what the drawing power of a crowd was, in simpler terms – the power of social proof. The research concluded that 4% of the total number of passersby looked in the upward direction when only one man looked up. Then, the same experiment was done again. The only difference was that in place of just one, this time, five men were looking up, and the percentage of people doing the same thing shot up to 18%. Similarly, when the number of people looking up was raised to 15, a greater increase was seen. The percentage of people behaving in the same way also increased and became 40% of the passersby. Even Cialdini had used this experiment to make his point about how powerful social proof can be.

Now, let us move on to some examples of social proof. If you look at life, you will find several incidents where one group of people is showered with several job opportunities while there is another group that cannot seem to find any job at all. The people who are struggling keep sending their resumes to every HR possible, but on the other hand, the others have already impressed a lot of recruiters. Similarly, one group of people keep dating one person after the other, but there are others who couldn't even find one person for them. But do you know why such unfortunate inequality prevails? The answer lies in social proof.

When society knows someone to be talented, successful, or attractive, these views keep spreading from one person to another very quickly. But when there is no social proof about a person, people become attentive to the flaws. Even when the qualifications of two people are the same when it comes to a key role, the person who already has a job in the high ranks is preferred. Similarly, even if two writers have the same qualities and are equally talented, publishing a book will be much less of a hassle for the person whose first book was a bestseller. The list keeps going on in the same manner.

Now, here is a real-life example of social proof. This example concerns the Petrified Forest in Arizona. The people going to the forest were stealing the petrified wood, and it was increasingly becoming a serious issue. So, a sign was put up by the authorities that said – "The natural state of the forest has been destroyed by those who had stolen the petrified wood in the past." The aim of putting up this sign was to create awareness among the public so that the theft can be minimized. But exactly the opposite happened. The theft increased, and in fact, it became thrice of what it used to be. Experts analyzed this issue, and they came to the conclusion that the signs actually served as social proof that stealing from the Petrified Fores can be justified.

Nowadays, influencer marketing is completely based on the concept of social proof. When someone you prefer is using a product or service, you automatically see that thing in a different light, and it becomes desirable to you. This effect is also popularly known as the 'halo and horns effect.' Similarly, you will often see that night clubs imply their popularity by keeping patrons waiting outside their doors. It leads to a feeling of desirability among others and increases their popularity.

Chapter 3: How to Identify a Manipulator?

Manipulation is something that we have all dealt with, but it is not as easy to identify as it seems. Yes, sometimes, even though people are manipulating you, it won't harm you in any way. But on several occasions, manipulation can have severe consequences because the manipulator might have some selfish motives.

Think about it – did you ever feel someone is trying to control you or pressurize you into doing something that you don't want to do? It can be with someone you are involved in a close relationship or even a run-in with some acquaintance of yours. Manipulation can be of different types – it can be your emotionally abusive partner, or it can also be a salesperson who is incessantly trying to sell you something that you don't want to buy. Therapists define manipulation as a strategy that is primarily an unhealthy psychological practice, and it is implemented by those people who want to get things their way and yet don't have it in them to ask for it directly. The tactics used by a manipulator are abusive and deceptive. But in some cases, you might not recognize manipulation right away because the manipulator acts in a friendly way in order to put their ulterior motive under a veil. In these cases, the victim is not able to realize that someone is manipulating them.

It becomes harder to spot a manipulator even more for those who have grown up in households where manipulation was a usual thing. Even though you might feel angry from time to time, but the manipulator will use feelings like sympathy and try to reason with you on the surface, and so, gradually, your instincts are overridden by these fake pleasantness of the manipulator. Manipulation tactics are very often used by codependent people mainly because they do not know how they can be assertive or direct about their feelings. So, in order to get what they want, they use manipulation. On the other hand, codependent people are also very easy prey for other manipulators, especially narcissists.

In this chapter, I am going to explain some traits to you that will help you identify a manipulator.

They Always Use the Victim Card

Most expert manipulators will make you feel guilty about one thing or the other. They take the help of constant victimization. In fact, they probably bring up a difficult phase of their life from time to time and play the 'trauma wild card' in front of you whenever they feel that they can't get things their way. After that, they also try to use that traumatic experience to justify anything bad that they have done. It can be anything like the death of a family member, traumatic childhood, abusive ex-partner, and so on. There is a certain level of inflated pride in the way they display their emotional scars, and you will automatically feel the vibe. They simply love to brag about whatever wrong that has happened in their life.

When someone poses to be the victim in all situations, they do experience some advantages over others, the major one being no one is going to criticize them. Moreover, everyone tries to understand their situation, empathize with them, and treat them with compassion. The moment someone questions them, that person would be declared as insensitive. So, they can hide behind their trauma, and people will automatically accept that whatever they are saying is true. But it has been often noticed that when someone is playing this victim card over and over again, they are actually hiding blackmail. I will not disagree with you that sometimes, there are cases where people are truly victims of some situations, but that doesn't mean that their state of being a victim is going to last forever.

So, how can you identify whether someone is really a victim or just a victim manipulator? Well, here are some of the things that you should look out for–

- The manipulators will not ask for anything directly, but they do have wants that they want to satisfy. So, they say something that is regretful or in the form of a complaint. For example, – 'Nobody understands my pain and the hurdles I have crossed.' When someone says this, it's easy for a person to get confused when the victim is trying to ask you for help, or are they simply angry at the fact that it was not as difficult for you as it was for them.
- If someone is trying to be manipulative, then you will experience a feeling of guilt every time you are with them. No matter what conversation you are having, they will make you feel that you have a role to play in their misery and so you should be guilty of it. All of this sadness emanating from the manipulator will put you in discomfort.
- When someone is a victim manipulator, they will often keep reminding you of the evil motives in every people around you. But when it comes to their own misdeeds, they will use the 'trauma card' to justify their ac-

tions. If you go on to criticize them as a hypocrite, they will call you callous and insensitive. And no one wants to hear these things, so victim manipulators use this as their weapon.
- These manipulators also have the habit of making sacrifices even when no one asked them to. After that, they will keep boasting about everything they did for you.

They Use Subtle Threats

Emotional blackmail or subtle threats is another thing that will help you spot the manipulators. It can be in the form of various things like shame, intimidation, or even rage. The threats they will make might not always be directly hurled at you. Sometimes they are subtle and indirect, but nonetheless, they are threats, and it is, in fact, a very commonly used tactic. Be it domestic abuse or huge political leaders; every manipulator has used threats at some point or the other. The main thing about this tactic is that the manipulator will openly tell you about the worst outcome that can happen and then pose it to you as a threat. For example, 'If you don't curb your eating, no one is going to date you because, in a few months, you will look like an elephant.' So, even if you give them any scientific information, they are simply not going to hear from you. This kind of behavior might be a result of several things. For example, if someone is not happy because you are eating pizza and they cannot because they are on a strict diet, they might manipulate you into not eating pizza as well. But the problem is, these people don't know how to say things directly, and so they hide behind toxic manipulation. They think that if they imply that a catastrophe will happen if you don't listen to them, then you will do as they say.

They Question Your Sanity

Another very notable characteristic of manipulators is that whenever you are in an argument with them, they will say something or do something that will make you question your sanity. In other terms, they use gaslighting. For example, if you narrate an incident to them, do they believe at one go, or do they question you regarding whether all the facts were correct? Do they believe your side of the story, or do they change the narration and make it seem that everything was your fault? If you are going for the latter part of each of these questions, then it is clear that you are dealing with a manipulator who uses gaslighting tactics to get what they want.

A manipulator is using tactics of emotional abuse if he/she is trying to gaslight you. There are so many adverse effects of gaslighting on the mental health of the victim because it leads to severe anxiety and can even lead to panic attacks and nervous breakdowns in the future. Here is a list of things that happens if you are with a manipulative person who is trying to use gaslighting to gain the upper hand –

- Whenever you have a conversation with them, they will try to make you feel that you are making a big deal out of nothing. They will tell you that your emotions are all over the place and that you should learn to keep them in check. As a direct result of all this, you will slowly start thinking whether your feelings are justified or not.
- You will often find the manipulator pointing it out to you that the way you are dictating the events of the past are not the way they happened. When this happens, you will automatically start questioning your own memory. The manipulator does that so that they can change the narration of the past event to their own benefit.
- When you have a manipulator in your circle who is gaslighting you, you will automatically find yourself apologizing way too much. Whenever there is a confrontation or

an argument, you will feel the need to say sorry even though you were not the one at fault.
- You will find that your well-wishers, friends, or family might not like the manipulator, and you will incessantly want to defend that person in front of others. When you can't make them understand, you will start hiding things about the manipulator and paint the best picture possible in front of your acquaintances. But you are already aware of how unacceptable the behavior of the manipulator is, but somehow you are ashamed of it, and so you don't want to reveal the details.
- Gradually, after a certain point of time, you might even start feeling that something is definitely wrong with you, or you might have started to become crazy. If you are in a relationship with the manipulator, then you might also feel that it is because of you that the relationship is in tatters and that you are never going to be enough.
- The manipulator will make you doubt and second-guess yourself at every stage of your life, and you become so confused that you start to trust the judgment of others more than yours. You will also falter when it

comes to making decisions because you are no longer sure about your own judgment.
- You will no longer be the confident person you were before. Even though you have a gut feeling about the person manipulating you, you will not speak up about it because you are afraid or are facing self-doubt about this as well.

They Use Sarcasm to Devalue You

Manipulators will often try to devalue you, and they do this with the help of sarcasm. Like I told you before, manipulators don't know how they can engage in direct communication, and so, they use different tactics to get what they want, and undermining and insulting the person with sarcasm is one of them. With these sarcastic comments, they will make you feel as if you don't have any feelings or that your actions don't matter at all. The aim of the manipulator is to make you feel that you are inferior, and they want to put you in a position where you feel inferior.

One very common example that shows how sarcasm is used in manipulation is when someone sends you a message that seems friendly at a glance. But if you read between the lines, you will find there is aggressive content that is meant to insult you. For example, 'If you only went to a prestigious university, today you would have been living the life of your dreams.' So, by saying this, they are trying to say that you are not successful and you don't lead a quality life because you are not educated enough.

When someone has been manipulated for too long, they fail to recognize this kind of behavior as manipulation. It is because they think that the other person actually has their best interests in mind, and so they are trying to help them out. But what you need to understand is that making you feel bad about yourself is not the way of helping you. It is insulting, and it will only push you further into a cycle of self-loathing. If someone wants to give you some useful advice, then they will engage in direct communication, and they won't be devaluing you. Making jokes that are insulting and makes you feel inferior is not a way of showing respect.

They Are Control Freaks

Like I told you before, manipulators are abusive and toxic, and they are also control freaks. But they do their best to hide their control-freak nature. In fact, when people become experts at manipulation, they often mask their control-freak attitude with love. For example, if your partner buys you a dress that is one size smaller and tells you that he did it only because you can wear it once you lose weight because you'd look so good when you do. See, this behavior right here is an example of manipulation. The person doesn't bother to ask you whether you want to lose weight or not. They didn't even have a proper conversation with you. They simply came up with a manipulative idea to force you into losing weight. He has this idea of the perfect woman he wants to be with, and so, using kind words that have a motive behind it, he wants to mold you into his idea of 'perfect.' That's exactly what manipulation is.

Control freak nature can also be spotted when a person has been isolating you from all others in your life. In simpler words, they have been keeping you all to themselves. They made all the plans and did not bother to ask you. They take it for granted that you are going to be okay with whatever plan they make. So, before you can even realize you become isolated from all the people that you love. And you keep relying on the manipulator so much, that gradually, you start losing your close ones. If the person has a habit of becoming angry at you from time to time, you might find them apologizing, but those apologies don't really hold any meaning whatsoever because they repeat the same mistakes again.

In fact, when someone promises you that they are not going to do the same thing twice, it gives you hope that maybe things are going to change for the better. But when they don't, whatever self-esteem you had goes away because of all the harsh words the manipulator hurls at you.

They Always Think About What Is Good For Them

Manipulators are not in the habit of having your best interests at heart. They care only about their personal gain, no matter what happens to the other person. One of the characteristic traits of any manipulator is that they always try to keep the victims dependent on them. They will twist your actions and thoughts by using different tactics so that in the end, you cannot do anything without the manipulator's advice or consent. You will slowly be molded into a person who doesn't have a purpose but does everything that will somehow benefit the manipulator. So, the only person that the manipulator thinks of is themselves. You will slowly reach a point where you no longer have faith in yourself, but you trust the manipulator more. Everything that a manipulator does serves them in some way or the other. It is never meant to benefit you even though on the outside, the manipulator might sugar-coat everything they say. How your actions are impacting your life is of little or no interest to the manipulator.

When you have a positive bonding with someone, they will help you grow. On the contrary, if there is a manipulator in your life, no matter what relationship you share with them, they will always point you out your flaws and shortcomings. Also, they will constantly tell you that you can indeed overcome those shortcomings if you take their help. In that way, you can do well, which means that you have to stay dependent on the manipulator. This is also how the victim is convinced that whatever the manipulator is telling them is for their own good.

They Will Constantly Blame You For Everything

Playing the blame game is a constant trait of every type of manipulator you will ever meet. There is no limit to the amount of blame they can put on their victims. Be it their actions or something they had said, the manipulators will figure out a way to blame their victims for even the smallest of things. Moreover, if the victim tries to tell the manipulator that they have done nothing wrong, the manipulator will immediately turn the tables and, in some way or the other, make the victim look pitiful and selfish. Their lying words are so strong that they will make it possible for the victim to prove anything to them. They will put everything on the victim, saying that they cannot remember details or they have forgotten what exactly had happened.

Eventually, when things go on like this for a long time, the victim slowly starts to question their version of the events, and this makes them feel anxious. They feel sorry that they had even tried to challenge the manipulator in the first place. So, as you can understand, no matter what, you cannot make the manipulator own up to their faults. It happens even more when admitting to what they have done puts them at a disadvantage. In fact, whenever something happens, the manipulator will always try to find someone on whom he/she can pin everything.

Moreover, another trait of manipulators is that they are in the habit of keeping score of what you are doing every day. They will bring things up one day and spew out all the mistakes they have been keeping score of. They will start blaming you for all those things, no matter how insignificant they are. Yes, there are times when the manipulator might be eager to help, but that help is never without a price tag. Even if they help you out only once, they will keep bringing up that one instance to get favors from you and keep manipulating you so that you have this constant feeling of being indebted to the manipulator.

Their Mood Changes Very Frequently

The manipulator is always wearing this invisible mask. They never show their real self. So, whatever behavior they are showing in front of you is nothing but a façade. When they want something from you, you will see that they are on their best behavior. But when they realize that you have now become totally dependent on them and they can control you emotionally, they will test you by pulling back. Manipulators love to see their victims squirm. Their mood keeps changing so frequently throughout the day. It makes the victim even more uncomfortable because they can never be sure of the mood in which the manipulator will show up. That is why victims become even more vulnerable to the manipulation tactics because they don't know when to put their guard up.

They also give positive compliments, but with every compliment, there will be something negative. This is called negging because the victim starts to bond with the manipulator because of all the positive compliments. At the same time, the victim also faced a lot of emotional difficulties because of the constant criticism.

They Keep Changing Their Expectations

This is also very common among manipulators, and they do this on purpose. When the victim tries their best to please the manipulator, that is when the manipulator changes his/her expectation. In this way, the victim feels that no matter how hard they try, the manipulator is never satisfied. It is like playing a board game with someone who keeps changing the rules after every turn so that there is no way for you to win. It always feels like an uphill climb that never ends. Moreover, the victim always feels like they don't have all the information required o make the decisions, and so, they feel that they always do something wrong.

So, if there is a person in your life who makes you feel confused at all times, then it is probably because they are manipulating you. If you are in a healthy relationship, it is never meant to feel confusing. Do you know why manipulators keep changing what they want? It is because they know that their victims want to please them so much that they are going to go to any extent to fulfill their expectations.

So, these were some of the signs that will help you identify a manipulator. Always remember that knowledge is power, and when you are aware of what it looks like to be with a manipulator, it will automatically become easier to spot one.

Chapter 4: Ten Approaches Manipulators Use Emotional Intelligence as a Trap and How to Escape?

I am sure every one of you has heard of the term emotional intelligence by now because it has been doing round in the market for quite some time now. In the third part of this book, we will be dealing with emotional intelligence in detail. It was in the 1960s when the term was coined for the first time. In short, emotional intelligence is the ability of a person to identify the emotions a person is going through and then use that ability to make better decisions. Emotional intelligence is also often referred to as EQ or EI. It is not something that you can master in a day because it has to be cultivated over time. You have to work on it and sharpen it. But you have to keep in mind that even EQ can be used unethically, and that is what manipulators do.

No one wants to be manipulated, but every one of us has faced it in our lives. So, here are some of the approaches of EQ that is used by manipulators to set a trap.

They Use Fear

Fear is one of the greatest tools of any manipulator. Whenever they dictate some incident to you, they will not state the facts as they are but overemphasize and exaggerate certain things so that you get scared and take action based on that fear. Whenever fear is being used for manipulating a person, usually, the manipulator has a planned motive behind it. They always work towards their objective so that even the victim thinks that whatever the manipulator is doing has a reason behind it. In this way, guilt starts creeping in the hearts of the victims, and everybody else sees the manipulator as someone who is innocent and has nothing to do with the situation whatsoever.

Discrediting the victim or undermining them is what gives the manipulator the upper hand, and so the only thing on their mind is how they can meet their needs. So, even if the victim tries to say something in defense, the manipulator will either ridicule them or speak down to them to keep them shut.

So, if you ever come across someone in your life who is using statements that somehow is intended to make you fearful of them, you need to beware of those people. They are manipulating you. So, before you take any action whatsoever, you need to be sure that you have a proper grasp of the whole picture.

They Will Try to Deceive You

Manipulators are very deceptive, and they keep changing their nature very frequently. Honesty is something that is important in all types of relationships, but manipulators have no regard for honesty. They don't believe in transparency as well. In fact, they will go to extreme lengths to keep the truth hidden from their victims so that the manipulator always remains in control. It happens in the work environment too. Have you ever had to deal with an employee who was spreading falsified information regarding you just because those rumors are going to benefit them? Well, that is exactly what a deceptive personality looks like. So, in simpler terms, whenever someone is not giving you the full truth about something, and they are either exaggeration the facts or omitting certain things or distorting the events so that they can influence your decisions, it is called manipulation.

But, it is not easy to spot deceptive people. You have to be extremely observant. There might be some slips in their body language or the way they speak. You will learn more about these in the latter part of this book, where you will see how mismatched behavior is often a pointer for spotting deceptive people. So, whenever someone is telling you something, don't believe them right away, no matter how saint they look. You have to ask questions, sort out your facts, and get these from a reliable source. When you think that your details are not aligning in a proper line, you need to do some more digging. Base your decisions on the fact that you find and not on what someone else is suggesting you to do.

They Take Advantage of Their Victims When They Are Happy

Manipulative people have this target of taking advantage of their victims, especially when they seem to be happy. It is very common for humans to be ready to say yes to almost anything when they are in a chirpy and good mood. If any opportunity is presented to them at this moment, they won't be able to say whether it is really good or it has been just sugar-coated. So, they have a tendency to jump at these opportunities at once. But you have to take a stand and stop people from taking advantage of you all the time.

So, if you don't want people taking advantage of you, here are some things that you need to keep in mind –

- There will be countless times in your life when people might call in a favor or ask you to help them out with something. Should you say yes to them right away? Absolutely no! You should think about what they are asking you to do and think about it very carefully. Ask yourself whether you are being tempted to say yes, or do you really want to help that person? In short, think before you agree to do something. If you don't want to pose yourself as rude, then you don't have to be direct about it. You can subtly say no to the person. You can also say that you are going to get back to them in a few days because you need to think it over.

When someone is pressurizing you to do something, the chances are that you will make the wrong decision, but it is up to you whether you want to choose the right path.

- It is important to learn how to say no in different circumstances; otherwise, when manipulators find you happy, they are going to ask you to do things that you would have rejected in any other situation. I know that it can be intimidating and tough for anyone to say no, but if you don't give it a try at least once, you are never going to be sure. You don't have to start with something big. Start small so that you can gradually make yourself comfortable saying no.
- The next thing that you should do is define your limits and abide by them. If you find yourself in a situation where someone keeps asking you things you don't want to do, you have to set a limit for that person. For example, if someone you know is asking you to lend some money, be direct about it and tell them if the amount they are asking is too much for you. Similarly, if your boss is asking you to work extra time, then it is not that you have to listen to them at all times. Tell them politely that you already have

some plans of your own and that you cannot stay back.
- When you realize that someone is always taking advantage of your goodness, it really hurts. But that does not mean you won't do anything about it and allow the person to keep taking advantage of you. That is not how things work. If you can't figure out things by yourself, it is better if you talk to someone who you think will understand your position.
- Try to distance yourself from people who are taking advantage of you. Trust me; you don't need them in your life. If you are not comfortable with someone, there is no use of putting up with them on a daily basis.

They Misuse Your Trust

A manipulative person doesn't know how to respect your trust. They will use several coercive methods to get things their way. But you cannot back down and let them have it. At first, the manipulator might give you several compliments to gain your love and trust, and when you begin trusting them, they might ask for bigger favors. In order to do that, they can even exaggerate their version of events. I know that we are always taught to give others, and it definitely brings an immense about of joy, but you cannot keep giving to people to a point where you are draining yourself of all energy. It is important that you understand when you have reached the limit.

In the first part of the book, you already saw how reciprocity works, and now, you have to protect yourself from that same cycle of reciprocity so that the manipulator cannot use it against you.

Manipulators often become habitual liars. They will keep lying about the simplest things, and they will lie even when they don't have to do so. It becomes a habit for them. Through their lies, they want to make you confused so that you cannot find out about their true motives. In this way, they keep doing what they want, and the victim fails to notice their true colors. In fact, in severe cases, the manipulators use toxic tactics to put the victim on the defensive and hurl at them with several falsified accusations.

Sometimes, lying is not as direct as you think. It can also be in the form of indirect comments. They might not give you some material information willingly or be vague while explaining something important. This is also a part of lying. When confronted, they will say that whatever they told you was true, and this is how they act like saints. They tell you the truth, but they don't tell you all of it. For example, your partner might tell you that they are going to return home late, but what they are hiding is that they are having an affair, and they are going to be out on a dinner with the other person.

They Use Denial

Did you know that denial is also a manipulation tactic? And when I am talking about denial, I am talking about conscious denial and not the unconscious one where people deny a traumatic event. This type of denial is done consciously because the manipulator doesn't want to agree to the promises he/she made earlier, and they will deny having knowledge of any behavior that is manipulative.

Even when the victim tries to deal with it rationally or discuss things, the manipulator will always act like the victim is making a huge fuss out of nothing. They will instead say things that will make the victim doubt themselves. In the previous point, I already explained how they use lies to cover up their deeds. And when someone confronts them about those lies, they will instantly go into the denial mode so that no one can link them to the manipulative tactics.

They Have a Lot of Queries

You will often find manipulators questioning you regarding a lot of stuff. It is said that when someone asks you about yourself, it is easy to give answers because you already know everything about yourself. This is what manipulators use to their advantage. Every question that they are going to ask you will have some sort of hidden agenda in it. When they find the answer that shows your weakness or anything that they can use against you, they will make a mental note of it and then use that information later on to their own benefit.

But don't get me wrong – I am not asking you to have a suspicion on everyone you meet. Not everyone will have a hidden agenda, but many people will have it. If you have someone in your life who keeps pestering you with the same questions even when you have repeatedly told them that you don't want to answer it, those are the people you should be careful of. Also, there will be some people who will be unwilling to reveal anything when you ask the same question to them. This is because they know that answering the question is uncomfortable and if they know that, they shouldn't be asking you to do the same unless they have some hidden agenda.

They Try to Get the Best Out of Home-Court Advantage

If you don't know what home-court advantage means, let me explain it to you. It is basically a space where a person feels he is comfortable in and can be confident while speaking to another peson. Manipulators always try to have the conversation in a space in which they have the home-court advantage. So, you will often find them pushing you to meet them at a physical space of their choice. This is because they know that they have the upper hand whenever they are in that space. They can exercise more control and dominance over you because of that space. The place gives them familiarity, and from that sense of familiarity, comes the feeling of dominance. Moreover, this place that the manipulator chooses is often a place where the victim feels uncomfortable, and this gives the manipulator a greater advantage.

So, if you want to deal with people who try to use this tactic and manipulate you into giving them what they want, I would suggest you do all kinds of conversations and negotiations at a place that seems neutral to you. But if you indeed have to meet the person at someplace where you are not comfortable, for example – their home, then you can first ask for a cup of coffee or a glass of water and get your mind at ease so that you can answer them intelligently. It will help you make better decisions.

They Have a Habit of Speaking Fast

If you think about it carefully, you will realize that there is nothing special when someone is talking fast. In fact, it has been found that when people try to speak fast, it is mostly because they are trying to hide something from the listener. Other times, it is mostly because there are completely clueless as to how they can communicate with you, and there are also times when people speak fast because they think they have a flaw, and they don't want others to notice it about them.

But it has also been observed that people who have the habit of fast talking, they also have much better skills at sales because they know how to manipulate your psychological state and make you feel that there is an urgency. It is very simple indeed – You will find if you can keep the person thinking throughout your conversation. Let us say you have gone to the showroom to buy a car, and you are already feeling a tad bit intimidated. The salesperson talking at a fast pace only increases the urgency, and you feel like inquiring about the car right away. But if you feel uncomfortable by those fast-paced conversations, don't step back from playing hardball.

Along with this habit of talking fast, manipulators also try to give their victims too many details so that they are totally confused about the situation. But if you have spoken with someone who tried to intimidate you with details, you need to ask yourself whether the person did it unintentionally or intentionally. In such situations, you sometimes even have to ask the person to slow down a bit so that you can listen to the story once more and try to understand the details. When you get details that don't add up, you have to spend a lot of your time patching them up and figuring out what really happened. It is not only time-consuming but also irritating.

So, the next time you come across someone who was being very expressive during the conversations, giving you too many details and confusing you, you need to state it clearly that they need to slow down. If you don't speak up, the manipulator will keep taking advantage of you.

There are also some manipulators who speak in a difficult language. They are simply so much verbose that it becomes difficult for the listener to keep up with what he/she is saying, and this, too, leads to a sense of urgency. Then, there are some manipulators who keep talking in circles to mislead the victim. For example, the person might keep repeating the same incident over and over again.

They Twist Every Story They Tell

Manipulators will never give you a straight answer or tell you something in a simple way. Their storytelling skills are really very good. The intent behind telling you a story is always that they want you to visit that particular situation in a certain way. The stories told by a manipulator are usually revolving around one single goal or person. And they are experts at making you see things through their eyes and the moment the manipulator is able to do that to a victim, that is when the sense of urgency is created.

For example, suppose one of your colleagues is telling you how her boyfriend broke up with her and how much she loved him. And after a few minutes, she starts crying. What would be your immediate response? You will go and comfort her in any way you can. I am not saying this is wrong – it will be okay if you have a very trustworthy relationship with that person, but in other cases, these situations usually have a manipulative intent.

They Give You Limited Time in Everything

In the last two points, we already spoke about the fact that manipulators love to create an ambiance of urgency for their victims. This is because whenever things seem urgent, the victim is not able to think much about it and relies on the manipulators regarding what they should do. And in that instance, the manipulators will try their best to swing your decisions in their favor. You will have to make an important decision in a time span that is unreasonably less. This is because the manipulator will not want you to weigh out the consequences of your actions and coerce you into making a choice that works well for them.

If you have met a person in your life who tries to create a situation like this, then you have to make it a resolution in your mind that you cannot submit to any demands that person is making until and unless you think it through. If the person doesn't agree to give you more time to think about an important matter, then you are better off without that person in your life. And if that person is your superior at work, then you have to stand your ground and tell them that you need more time because there is nothing wrong with it.

In all these points, I have also explained how you can go against the manipulator in each approach they make. But sometimes standing up is not so easy as it seems. The manipulator might even give you silent treatment just because you stood up to them. They will make you wait, and this is what gives them power because uncertainty and doubt will start creeping into your mind. So, if you think that the manipulator is going along the lines of giving you the silent treatment, try to make some communication but only up to a certain point of time. After that, you have to set a deadline and ask them to make some communication by then, or you are done with them.

Remember that there will always be manipulators around you, but you need to work on yourself and increase your level of emotional awareness so that you can deal with these manipulators. There is nothing better than sharpening your own emotional intelligence skills, and you will learn about it in-depth in Part 3 of this book.

Chapter 5: Myths of Hypnosis

We have all heard about hypnosis at some point or other in our lives, and I am sure that many of you have misconceptions about it. The public has known about hypnosis for quite a long time now, and during this span, it has given birth to several fantasies. Both news reporting and fiction media have helped in spreading these rumors. In fact, I know that most of you have heard that once someone has been hypnotized, it is quite difficult to bring them out of that state. They go into a 'trance,' and there is nothing that can be done. Or, you must have heard that hypnotism also works when someone is made to get triggered by a word, and then, they go into a zombie-like state. If an antidote is not found, then it's next to impossible to find a solution, and the person has to be kept locked up in a room forever.

Then there are myths about being possessed by a demon, losing your personality, losing your mind, and so on, but not a single one of them is sensible. They are all rubbish, and yet people believe them because they have been popularized over the ages. These things do not have any proof because they never happened. If you talk to anyone who has been hypnotized, they will tell you that the experience is nothing like this. These are all myths, and in this chapter, we are going to bust some of these common myths. I have tried my best to bust these myths with a proper explanation so that you don't feel like listening to gibberish.

Myth #1 – Hypnotism Can Be Done Only On People Who Are Mentally Weak

This is one of the biggest myths that is circulating, and I am telling you – this is not at all true. In fact, when a person is more intelligent, they have a better sense of self-control. These people can be hypnotized faster. So, the truth is quite the reverse of what the myth is. But do you know why? It is because being hypnotized is all about concentrating on a deeper level. You enter a stage where you are in a trance. So, if someone is already suffering from some mental health problem, being hypnotized can be difficult for them.

On the contrary, you should also understand that if you are not able to get hypnotized by someone, it doesn't mean that there is something wrong with your mental well-being. The susceptibility of people towards a concept like hypnosis is not same for everyone. It differs from one person to the other. In fact, studies have been conducted over the years, and all of them pointed out to the fact that almost 30% of the total population of people are comparatively quite resistant to the process of hypnosis. But if you keep giving continuous effort into it, you can get hypnotized. So, at the end of the day, it is the concentration power, willingness, and motivation of the person being hypnotized that determines whether he/she can be hypnotized or not. You can get the rewards if you are willing to work towards it.

Also, if your IQ is above 70, it is generally accepted that you can be hypnotized.

Myth #2 – People Who Can Hypnotize Others Have Special Powers

Hypnotism is not a magic show. It is based on scientific evidence, and so, the hypnotist doesn't have any special powers. This myth has often been spread into the masses through fiction movies. But this is not true – the hypnotists are real people just like you and me, and they do not possess any kind of special powers whatsoever. What is different is that they have studied human psychology in-depth, and so, they do understand the human psyche far better than you can I can. They do not have any special powers, but they have worked with a lot of people, and so now, they are experienced.

If someone is really enthusiastic about learning hypnosis and gives it sufficient practice over a period of time, then they can also hypnotize someone. But remember, you can hypnotize someone only if you have that person's consent to do so. Also, if you do learn hypnosis, it is always advised that you use the process to help others and not in a negative way.

Myth #3 – When People Are Hypnotized, They Become Helpless

This is yet another myth that needs to be busted. Many people have this idea that whenever someone is hypnotized, they move into a mindless state where they do not have any control whatsoever. The truth is that the morals of the person being hypnotized play a huge role here. It is extremely difficult for even an expert hypnotist to make someone do a task that is against their usual moral conduct.

In short, being hypnotized is not about allowing someone to control your mind. No one can do that until you willingly let that person control you. A hypnotist can merely make some suggestions, and these suggestions are usually based on an interview that you have with the hypnotist before the session. Your mind will always be yours – you won't be losing control over it during the session. For example, let us say that the hypnotist has suggested you to do something that you don't want to do. Your subconscious mind will immediately become aware of it and not let you do it despite you being in a hypnotized state. That being said, I would also tell you something else – when someone is hypnotized, it is possible for the hypnotist to reduce the person's inhibitions so that when a suggestion is provided to them, they are more eager to accept it.

Myth #4 – Hypnosis is Similar to Sleep

Let me tell you something very clearly – being hypnotized and sleeping is two completely different things, and there is no similarity between the two. People often get confused because when someone is hypnotized, they are in a peaceful state, and their eyes remain closed. But simply closing their eyes does not mean that they are asleep. Even when the brain waves are checked at this point, they differ to a great extent. There is no similarity in the waves for a person who is asleep and someone else who is hypnotized. In fact, if you check the EEG reports, you will see that when a person is in a hypnotic trance, their alpha waves are considerably greater. The higher these waves, the more alert and responsive the hypnotized person is. Whatever is happening in the surroundings of the hypnotized person, he/she is aware of it.

Myth #5 – You Will Have to Do Embarrassing Things

There are no embarrassing acts involved in hypnosis. But if you look at Hollywood fiction, this myth has been reinforced time and again, and that is why people believe it so strongly. But in the end, it is nothing but a myth. If you have got the idea after witnessing some stage hypnosis shows, then let me tell you something – in those shows, people do those things because they have volunteered to do so. Have you heard of hypnotherapy? It is basically a kind of therapy that's done with the help of hypnosis. But, it is not for entertainment – it is a serious method used to cure others' problems.

Myth #6 – You Just Need One Session of Hypnosis to Get Cured

Sometimes these advertisements claim that you will get cured with just one session from a hypnotherapist. But these are baseless, and hypnosis doesn't work that way. These claims are nothing but outrageous. There are so many imposters nowadays who will claim a lot of things, but they cannot achieve them. This myth has its origin in these imposters and even acts performed on stage.

But you will still hear people talking about how simply one session to a hypnotist solved all their problems, but is that true? No. Then why do they keep repeating? It's simply because it's a good story, and everyone will love to hear it.

If you want the trust, then here it is – a single session of hypnosis can never cure you. Reputed hypnotherapists always say that some people need as much as 20 sessions while others may get their solution in just 6 sessions. It varies from one person to the other, but a single session is never the solution. Think about it – change at this level cannot happen overnight – you have to give it some time. Even after that, hypnotherapy, all by itself, is rarely a solution to anything. You will have to get yourself involved in some other kind of treatment and use hypnotherapy as a supplementary treatment to get a solution. It is rarely the main method.

Myth #7 – It is Black Magic That Gave Rise to Hypnosis

First of all, I would like to remind you that there have been tons of scientific studies on hypnosis, and it has been extensively studied, unlike Black Magic, which is mainly based on superstitions. Palm readers and psychics are not the same as hypnotists. There are years of research behind hypnotism, and the names of several renowned psychologists are involved in this. For example – Dr. Carl Jung and Dr. Sigmund Freud. Some of the recent names in this field are that of Dr. John Kappas and Dr. Milton Erikson.

Myth #8 – The Patient Becomes Dependent on the Hypnotist After the Session

Absolutely not! When you are hypnotized, you are fully aware of that, and there will be times when you will be full control of yourself. Like I told you before, if the hypnotist even asks you to do something spontaneously, and if it goes against your moral policies, you can totally say no to the hypnotist. This is also why you should carefully choose your hypnotist before agreeing to work with them. The good hypnotherapists always ensure that their clients feel empowered during the session. They shouldn't be uncomfortable or feel that someone is authoritative. If the situation is more like the latter, then problems are inevitable, and the patient will not be able to get anything good out of the session.

Myth #9 – Hypnosis Can Help You Remember Memories That You Have Forgotten

I know that there are many of you who think this is true, but it's not. I do not deny it completely because there have been a few cases where this was possible. But there is no absolute guarantee that the hypnotists will succeed in helping you with this. Your subconscious mind is where your permanent memory resides. And the main idea behind hypnosis is using the information that is available in a person's subconscious mind. But you also have to remember that your memories are delicate and fragile. The emotional state of the person and their age has to be taken into consideration when you are trying to recover lost memories.

If the memory you are trying to retrieve is not being available at once or in simpler words, it is not readily available; there is good reason behind it. Your subconscious mind does it to hide some memories from your conscious self to avoid further trauma.

Myth #10 – I Have Never Been Hypnotized

Now, I know most of you are going to get surprised at this explanation, but it is quite common. It is said that every person will be hypnotized or enters that stage of trance at least two times every day. Do you know when? It is right before you wake up for the day in the morning and at night when you go to sleep. Moreover, there is another concept called environmental hypnosis, and it happens when you are reading a good book, and you are truly immersed in it, or you are watching an engrossing movie.

So, here are some of the common myths that I have debunked for you. But apart from what I already mentioned, here is something you should know – the sessions of hypnotherapy are completely private. So, if you are wondering whether you can use hypnotherapy to make people confess, it is not going to reach the court because it is inadmissible. Never confuse hypnotherapy with the tests done by the lie detector. Hypnotherapy can never make anyone confess or tell the truth forcefully. Also, there is no such thing as a miracle in this process. Like every other thing, you have to give it some time to see substantial progress.

Also, if you have not been under the supervision of a professional, do not try self-hypnosis. Without proper training, it can be detrimental and dangerous. You'll never realize how you will end up ingraining a negative thought in your mind. Moreover, self-hypnosis can never help you to reach out to your subconscious mind – that can be done only by a hypnotherapist.

Chapter 6: How to Hypnotize a Person?

If you are at this chapter, then you have already gone through the previous chapter, where I have debunked all the myths related to hypnosis. It is important for you to clear all your misconceptions because without that, you won't be able to take in any new knowledge. If this is your first time, I can understand how intimidating it must be for you, but don't worry, because we are going to see everything from the basic level here. The internet will burst you with tons of information, and all of that makes it worse for a person to figure out where to start, but here, you are going to get a crash course on how you can hypnotize a person. If what I have just said sounds interesting and that you'd love to learn a new thing, then go on and keep reading.

Making someone enter a trance-like situation is not that difficult, but let us start with the basics first.

What Do You Mean By a Hypnotic Trance?

Now, firstly, you need to understand that hypnosis is nothing but a state of mind that is completely natural. But people often get confused about the meaning of the word 'trance'. It is not any kind of spell or mythical state. Even though a lot of curiosity is doing rounds around this word, I am going to explain this to you in the simplest way possible.

If we are talking from a scientific point of view, then 'trance' is nothing but a metaphor. For a person to be hypnotized, they do not have to be in a trance. It is not synonymous. In order to study this state of mind, fMRI scans were done by researchers and the activity in the brain at that point was something like this –

- Self-reflection was less (because of lower activity in the region of the brain that is concerned with this function). In simpler words, the person was much less self-conscious.
- The part of the brain that is responsible for organization and planning was quite active.
- The person becomes free of all worries and enters a relaxed state of mind because of a reduction in activity in the dorsal anterior cingulate.

So, hypnotic trance is basically a state when the person will be more susceptible to accepting your suggestions. That is also the function of a trance. When you put someone in a trance and then shower them with plenty of suggestions, it is possible to make them think about adopting those suggestions in their life. So, in order to hypnotize someone, trance is simply a technique. It is not the be all and end all of the hypnosis.

Now, let us look at the different elements of hypnosis that will help you put a person in that state.

Induction

The first step of hypnosis is definitely induction. This is when you bring the person in the state of trance. There are three major things that are needed to be done to make it possible.

Firstly, you have to garner the attention of the person. Since hypnosis requires the person to increase their concentration level, you have to make them place their attention on you and not on the ongoings of the outside world. After that, the switch would be possible where they will slowly go from their conscious state to the subconscious state. There are various ways in which you can attract someone's attention. One of the easiest ways to do so is to ask them to look at you directly in the eyes. You can also show them a photograph on which they can concentrate or narrate a soothing story that will bring their attention to you.

But if you are in an informal setting, you can simply walk up to a person and initiate a conversation. Make sure you are polite and don't be too pushy; otherwise, you will just steer people away. But let us say that your subject is right in front of you. You have to start by asking them to close their eyes. Once they do that, tell them to enjoy a state where they are in a trance. Here is something worth noting – you should not only tell them to close their eyes but somehow also show that the process of closing one's eyes and going into a state of hypnosis is connected. This is how you get that person's attention.

Secondly, you have to bypass their conscious mind. Do you know what a person's conscious mind is? It is basically that voice in the head that often tells a person to reject things, accept them, or make a decision. Even though decision-making is so important, there comes the point where this process of decision-making becomes too complicated, and the person is stuck. That is where the importance of the unconscious mind comes in. Your unconscious mind is not in the habit of over-analyzing things like the conscious mind. It won't perform an evaluation of your judgments. If you ask it to do something, it would simply obey your command and get the work done. And hypnosis is all about communicating with the person's unconscious mind.

So, if you want to bypass the conscious and reach out to the unconscious mind, there are so many things that you can do, and this includes – telling a story that is engaging or using power words. Both of these approaches will help the person to imagine a world in their heads. They can listen to all the facts and then connect the dots. Also, make sure whatever you are saying is full of emotional content. One of the best ways to get started in this respect is by narrating a story. No matter what the age of the person is, captivating him/her is possible if you are a good storyteller. It can be anything – some story you heard in your childhood or even a story that you made up just now.

Thirdly, you have to stimulate the person's unconscious mind. This is the last step of the induction process of hypnosis. If the person whom you are hypnotizing is already enthralled by the story you are narrating, then you have done a great job because their unconscious mind starts to get stimulated. It is the power of the unconscious mind of a person that is utilized in hypnosis so that the person can start believing in their abilities again and lead a life that if fulfilling. The induction has to be done on a theme that the person struggles with. For example, if you are working with a person who is a workaholic, then their major problem is that they do not know how to rest. In that case, you have to make the induction session based on relaxation. It all depends on the person's susceptibility to the process of hypnosis. Those who are more susceptible are easier to deal with and can be induced within a few minutes, but with others, you might have to spend a bit more time.

Give Hypnotic Suggestions

Now that you have completed the first step of the process that is, induction – it is time for you to move on to the second step. In this step, you are going to give some hypnotic suggestions to the person to change their thought or try to change some of their habits. This suggestion can be anything or everything. For example, if, during the trance, you are asking the person to keep their focus on your voice, that is a hypnotic suggestion as well. These types of suggestions are usually used when the person is taken into a deeper state of hypnosis.

Then, there are directive suggestions as well. Let us say; you have asked the person to think about the taste of cigarette leaves in their mouth and feel how disgusting they taste. After that, you can suggest them to think about this taste whenever they feel the urge to smoke. This is how gradually you can help someone overcome their smoking habits.

But there is a prerequisite of this phase that needs to be done before you even start this process. You have to sit with the person and ask them a few questions that will help you determine the goal of the overall suggestions. In this way, you can work with the person and come up with suggestions that are going to help/her to a great extent. Since this step of hypnosis is all about stimulating the person's imaginary senses, you have to allow your imagination to flow as well. Whenever you are describing something, you should be vague about it – you don't have to provide them with too many details. This will give the person their chance to fill up the landscape in their mind with details of their choice. But you narrating this suggestion once won't help. You have to keep repeating the suggestions to the person over and over again. If you want any change, repetition is very important.

Guide the Person Out of the Trance

Finally, coming to the last step of the process – this is where you help the person come out of the state of trance. This will bring them back to the waking state they were previously in. This part is very simple. You can tell them that you are going to count till 3 and they have to bring themselves out of the trance by then. You should also tell them that once they open their eyes, they are going to feel relaxed and refreshed.

Here is something that you should keep in mind before you bring someone out of the state of trance – if there had been any suggestions that you don't want the person to continue in their real life, then you have to cancel those suggestions. After that, tell them that they can open their eyes and move their arms.

In some cases, you might find that the patient is acting reluctant to wake up. In that case, you should reassure the person that if they wake up, they are going to feel relaxed. Tell them that they can awaken, and it is completely okay. They will feel normal once they wake up, and when you are able to bring them back, ask them to do some casual stretches.

But if you want to be ethical about your practice of hypnosis, there are some points that you should keep in mind, and here they are –

- You can perform hypnosis only when your subject has full consent to it.

- When you bring your subject to a session, make sure they feel comfortable with the atmosphere. Thye must be physically safe. All of these things might seem insignificant now, but they are very much important if you want the person to wake up soon.
- Your intent behind performing hypnosis should not be malicious. You should not blackmail your friends or family.
- If someone is not ready for something that you are asked to do during the hypnosis session, respect their wish, and refrain from doing it.
- You should never hypnotize a minor.

Even after explaining everything in detail, I still want to remind you that hypnosis is very real, and it is not a magic trick that you get to witness at a local fair. Hypnosis can actually help people have a good sleep and release all the stress. Stress and anxiety are not good for your health, and they can be eliminated with the help of hypnosis. In fact, there are a lot of things that can derive help from hypnosis if it is used ethically.

Chapter 7: How Does a Hypnotherapy Script Work?

Following hypnotherapy scripts is a debatable issue, but first, let us see what these scripts mean. Basically, these are some scripts that are pre-made, and you can follow to hypnotize someone. The alternative to these scripts is to simply follow your intuition and say whatever you feel like saying at that moment. But even when you have a script in your hand, it is not 100% absolute that you will be able to execute them perfectly. So, in this chapter, we are going to have a look at some of the hypnotherapy scripts. Then we will move on to the tips that will help you derive the best out of these scripts.

Induction Script

This is the most commonly used script, and I have given you a brief idea of this in the previous chapter. Here, we are going to explore it a bit more. Here is a typical example of an induction script that will help you learn more about it –

The first part of the script will focus on how you can set up the person's expectation and also show them the inevitability factors:

I am going to guide you on how you can get into trance… how to take off stress from your mind and relax your body… and the way in which you will do this is really enjoyable…

Once you take the first step towards this process, nothing can stop you from going into the state of trance…

You don't have to make any extra effort… everything will simply happen on its own… all you have to do is keep following my instructions… and you will quickly go into a state of trance…

The second part of the script is helping the person relax their body, and towards the end, you are going to give them some reassurance as well.

Now, take a deep breath and try to relax... that's right... take another deep breath and slowly let it go...

Again, take a deep breath, and this time, close your eyes slowly... feel every muscle in your body relaxing when you are closing your eyes...

Keep breathing... allow the tension from your shoulders to release... shrug them... yes, that's right... now, loosen your hands and don't keep any tension in them...

Now, focus on your eyes... focus on the muscles of your eyelids... feel those muscles getting relaxed... and now they are so relaxed that you don't feel like opening them... continue with the relaxation... feel your eyelids becoming heavy... so tired... you cannot open them at all...

When you know that your eyes are completely relaxed, you won't be able to open them... because they are tired... and they just won't open... that's right... you can keep trying, but your eyes won't listen to you... don't panic, just keep enjoying the relaxed state...

Now, you are going to guide the person into a deeper state.

Feel the relaxation spread throughout your body...feel it like a wave...let go of every muscle holding you back...that's right...

Meanwhile, feel yourself going deeper and deeper...and then, this feeling can be deepened further...

After this, you are going to guide the person to move into the state of incremental hypnosis.

Now that you are deep into a state of relaxation, you can go way deeper than that. Take a deep breath, and after that, I will ask you to open your eyes slowly. After that, you are going to shut them back and move further deep into relaxation...if you feel that you can't open your eyes, it's alright...but try to open them in a while, and you will see that you can open them...when you close thos eyes again, feel your body going into a ten times deeper state of relaxation...you will go even deeper...yes, that's righ...ten times deeper.

Now comes the phase of instant hypnosis.

Make yourself feel comfortable in this state...you will be able to lift up your arm in a while...you don't have to do anything…just keep your arm limp and allow it to stay in the air…

Take one arm of the person and shake it a bit. It should be pliable and soft. It will give you an idea about the state of relaxation of the patient.

Now, I will slowly allow your arm to drop back down, and with every inch it drops, you will feel yourself going into a further deeper state of trance…keep going…yes, that's right…go deeper…

After this, you can carry on with the therapy at your pace.

Deepening Script

This type of script is often used in the induction phase, and it helps you to bring the person into a deeper state of relaxation. We have used this script in the previous example as well. If you want to make someone go deeper in their state of trance, here are some ways in which you can do it –

- The first step is to ask them to go into a deeper state, but the language you use should be presuppositional. For example, you can ask someone like this – 'In the next few seconds, you are going to go into a deeper state where you can find different ideas and images coming to your mind.' In simpler terms, you are asking the person to go deeper but not directly because you are shifting their focus to the benefits of going deeper. Whenever you are using the phrase – 'relax deeper into trance,' you are directly asking the person to go deeper, but even then, there is a permissive nature o the framework. If you want to make it more meaningful, try to say those things slowly.

- With some people, the deepening script can be taken to the next level. You can make the person feel that this whole idea of going deeper into the state of hypnosis is a phenomenon that is already present and, thus, is inevitable, and this can be done by hinting at it and linking it with the suggestion of going into a deeper state. This example should make it clearer to you – 'Breath out and in a few seconds, you will realize how further you can go into this hypnotic trance.' So, in this example, you can see how we are asking the person to experience something that we want them to experience, and this is made possible by forming a link between that and an experience that is definitely going to happen, that is, breathing out.
- The last technique that is want to share with you is the concept of creating worlds within

worlds. It is simply about creating different layers in consciousness. Each of these layers might represent different stages of the trance that the person is in. So, the first layer might be the stage of lightest trance, which can last only for a few seconds. After that, we move on to the state of parallel awareness, where the person is going deeper. But their focus is on both external and internal factors. So, even though their eyes are closed, they are still aware of the things going on in their surroundings. After that, comes the state where the main focus of the person in inwards. During this stage, whatever is happening in their surroundings is forgotten temporarily. In the deepest trance, all the therapeutic work is done.

Subject Script

The next type of script used in hypnosis is the subject script in which you can achieve your objective by giving different types of suggestions to the person in front of you. But whatever suggestions you make should be positive so that they are easily accepted by the person.

For example, if you are trying to talk to a smoker and make him/her realize that smoking is injurious to health. You do not tell them that directly. Instead of saying 'cigarettes cause cancer,' you can tell them 'imagine yourself quitting cigarettes and being a non-smoker for a year.' This is a more approach to handling the situation.

Termination Script

Next, we come to the final part where we are going to talk about the termination script or the awakening script. As you can understand from the term, this is the script used when you want to wake the person and end the trance. A usual awakening script will often start with you counting to five and then tell the person that their energy is going to come back. When you are narrating the termination script, make sure you also increase the energy in your voice slowly so that it helps the person come back to consciousness. Here is an example to help you understand better –

I will count from one to five, and then you will be able to open your eyes…you will be completely awake…and you will feel good…

One…you are slowly getting the feeling of coming back…two…the energy has started radiating throughout your body…feel the energy…three…try to move your toes and fingers…move them slowly…you will become more conscious but slowly…now, you will feel that the energy is flowing through your body faster…four…you will hear the sounds of everything that is happening in your surroundings…yes, take it slow…that's right…take the wakeful energy and feel it in your entire body…balance the energies…clear your head…you will feel good…five…slowly open your eyes…now, you will be coming back fully….you are fully back…your eyes are wide open…that's right…you've done well…you are wide awake…

Tips to Make the Best Out of the Hypnotherapy Scripts

If you want to get the best results from these scripts, then you also need to keep some things in mind. I have listed them below –

- The delivery of your script and your voice play a very important role in whether it will actually work or not. If you want the person to understand your point, then you need to keep in mind that you are not simply dictating a descriptive paragraph – this is not some to-do list. The inflections, pauses, pacing, and style should be appropriate to ensure the correct presentation. It is one of the most important points that you should

stress upon, and this also brings us to the next point.
- You shouldn't come across as someone who is reading a script. It won't have any effect on the person if you don't make it sound like you really mean what you say.
- Just because you came up with the idea of the words from a script, it doesn't mean that you won't try to understand what everything means. Every sentence should be clear to you because if you don't understand the meaning yourself, you won't be able to convey it clearly in your words. When you are reading a script that has been written by someone else, it might not match your style. Moreover, the script was not written with the person in mind. So, if you have to make some changes based on the person you are going to apply it on, then go ahead and make the changes. But you still have to make sure that everything is making sense.
- You also have to keep a close eye on the person in front of you. It will make sure that you can notice the signals or cues throughout the process. One of the most important things is to pay absolute importance to the person. If you are reading the script from a paper, keep it at a level that is at the same

level to the person's face so that you can look at them from time to time.
- One of the best approaches to get the most out of hypnotherapy scripts is that you can write the script in your own words. You have to keep the person in mind and rewrite the script accordingly. It is indeed one of the proven ways to make it more congruent. But have a template script ready with you that you can modify everytime you practice hypnotherapy with someone new. If you are a beginner at hypnotherapy, then a script is going to be a very effective tool for you only if you can use it wisely.

Chapter 8: A Brief Introduction to Mind Control

Mind control is a general term that is used to define various theories that propose that a person's decisions, emotions, behavior, or thinking can be influenced. Many genres of fiction use mind control as a common plot device. The fact that it is omnipresent is perhaps unsurprising. The prospect of being able to gain full and explicit control of the mind gives rise to many startling and alluring possibilities. There are several implausible forms of fictional mind control – magical interventions, telepathy, and evil plans of authoritarian organizations. Mind control is also implemented by certain devices in more scientifically-inspired plotlines where certain devices are implanted in the brain of the subject to manipulate neurophysiological processes that can cause a change of mental state.

In the real world, mind control involves various methods by which the mind can be influenced. It includes the effects that are mediated via our senses. These might include positive influences like using environmental manipulation to nudge someone to make healthy decisions or using presented evidence to update one's belief. They can also be subtler, as in the case of brainwashing or propaganda. Apart from environmental and social means, it can also be caused by direct neural stimulation. Neural stimulations can cause neural discharges through direct manipulations via brain stimulation or by subtle modulation with pharmacological agents. There has been a steady increase in the usage of brain stimulation in the last few decades as assistance to many suffering from mental disorders.

What is Mind Control?

The words "mind control" and "cult" have many misunderstandings regarding their definitions. But what do these words mean, and how can you tell the difference between being controlled into exploitation and the conveyance of a good idea?

Mind control is defined by several terms including compliance-gaining influence, behavioral change technology, sociopsychological manipulation, malignant use of group dynamics, exploitive persuasion, manipulation, and uninformed consent, thought reform, coercive persuasion, and brainwashing. Cults, on the other hand, are known by names such as ideological totalism, coercive organization, authoritarian structure, and closed system of logic. While some of these words are full of preconceived ideas, emotions, energy, and charge, others are more self-descriptive.

The study of thought reform is considered to be the study of the method of altering people's behaviors and minds through influence and persuasion. Influence is not inherently negative in and of itself. The degree to which a person is exploited and the extent of the deception used is what differentiates coercive persuasion from ethical persuasion.

A light form of coercive persuasion is television advertisements. Marketers often take advantage of the fact that when you are watching television, your mind is in a mild state of trance. They associate their products with some positive imagery that is completely unrelated. For instance, some of the persuasive images used by them are of puppies, babies, and sex. However, sometimes there is nothing relating the products to the images. Advertisers often make their products appear better than they actually are by bending the truth ever-so-slightly. On their own, these kinds of persuasive tricks are not really effective. Advertisements, however, most don't include love-bombing, shame, guilt, or fear tactics. Even if they are used, they are at low levels. Outright deception is prohibited by several laws, and a majority of companies convey the truth while informing their customers.

In contrast to this, a cultic group will make every possible effort to recruit and retain their members. These groups make use of different persuasive techniques in unison. Such methods strip the victim's real personality and form a new, group pseudo-personality. There is no method to avoid information control, deception, and lies. The new members who join the group don't know very much about the group or its purpose, or their expectations from the group. People start investing psychologically, spiritually, and emotionally, sacrifice a huge amount of money and time, and get deeply involved in the organization. It gets very difficult for them to leave the organization. Former members often struggle to regain their sense of sanity.

Persuasive techniques of mind control are everywhere around us, from activists, authors, scientists, religions, politicians, corporations, to family and friends. So, the actual question you should ask is whether you are being persuaded by open access to information, research, reason, and facts. Or are you persuaded by deceptive and manipulative methods? Consent that is gained through fraud is not real consent at all. The methods used by cults are also used in several dysfunctional families. An individual in an abusive marriage often faces similar experiences as someone in a cultic group.

Mind control vs. Brainwashing

Cults generally have the same basic patterns and ingredients, but there are various assorted styles and flavors of cults. Brainwashing has gotten refined into mind control since the Korean War and has become very common in the modern world. In order to be under mind control, an individual does not have to be subjected to any of the obvious abuses that are associated with brainwashing like be kept without sleep or food or be treated badly.

People learn on two different stages, the subconscious and the conscious. Even though some cults don't agree that there is a subconscious level, that is their main aim. For instance, activities like church services or seminars that last for one to two hours, create and make use of boredom. The subconscious mind is unguarded when the conscious mind starts to daydream because of boredom. Then, we are open to receive any messages that are being fed to us. Although this modern-day technique of hypnosis is mostly undefined, it is a recognized technique of mind control. The individual enters a state of hypnosis or trance, as is understood by those who study cults.

When an individual is aware of whom the person is, it is known as brainwashing. For instance, the Americans stuck in the Korean prison. The American boy can more easily work his way out of the situation and have an understanding of what had happened to him as he can recall where he was before his mind was changed through coercion. He can also identify the enemy who was involved in that "transformation" or "process."

Mind control is, however, done by someone that the person trusts. It could be a teacher of a seminar or class, or a minister, etc. It is very difficult to bring mind control to the attention of the victim as the techniques are usually very subtle. He cannot detect that someone else is controlling his mind as he thinks that he is in control of his behaviors as its happening completely out of his awareness. When he starts to realize that he has traveled from A to B but is unaware of where B is, it then dawns upon him. Mind control alters his view of reality and the whole world as well. He might even go through his whole life, failing to realize that he has been under mind control. He continues to view the world in the way that was shown to him by the cult and continues to refuse that he is not in full control of his own mind. He fails to realize that he needs help and thus is most hard to help. He will continue to be under mind control until something forces the people like him who are in the same cult to examine their belief system critically.

How to Take Control of Your Own Mind

Almost everyone has a negative voice inside their head. It is a part of life. Dealing with the negative thoughts that plague your mind day and night can help you grow and improve yourself to become a better version of yourself. Negative thoughts are a bit more manageable during the day as you are distracted by responsibilities, family, and work. However, the thoughts get louder when the night rolls in. It might get difficult to stop feeling helpless when you lose control. They might show up disguised as anxiety, doubt, or fear. Your imagination can get triggered by just a single small thought, and that can get you tumbling into a whirlwind that could knock you off. However, you can alter your thought process.

You can take back control through mind control. Mind control can improve the quality of your life. You can take back the control of your thoughts even though you might not be able to stop the initial trigger. Here's how you can get a grip on your thoughts:

- **Present moment mindfulness** – You require a mental support system when you are trying to take control of your thoughts. Present Moment Mindfulness can work fast. If you get caught in the whirlwind of negative thoughts, identify it, remove and replace it. Try to keep your focus on whatever you are doing at the moment. For example, if you feel your mind wandering off into a dark path while you are washing dishes, stop and notice your activity and tell yourself that you are washing the dishes. Feel the warm water and the soap bubbling on your hands.
- **Do a reality check** – When the cyclone of negative thoughts gets a hold on your imagination, you start believing whatever you are thinking. However, in reality, it is just what you have created in your mind. It's up to you to remove your thoughts and bring yourself back to the real world.
- **Erase and replace** – At times, it is just enough to remind yourself to "erase and replace." This positive mantra helps to create room for positive thoughts by kicking out the negativity. Having a "replace" statement ready for use might also help you when you need it. You just need one word. It could be "go," "no," "stop," or whatever you would

like. Repeat the word over and over again. You can be as creative as you wish – you can sing it, scream it, or chant it.
- **Name it –** When you feel stuck in a negative thought cycle, stop the cycle by naming it. Naming it creates a distinction in your subconscious mind whether you choose to say it out loud or whisper it. This will help to break the cycle.
- **Always be prepared –** Being aware helps you to be mentally strong enough to fight off the negative thoughts. When you are aware, you can identify the triggers and immediately knock it off. You can take back control by being more aware and grabbing hold of your mind.

Advantages of Mind Control

Mind control is a very effective form of persuasion. It is exponentially more accurate and powerful than other methods of persuasion. One of the most important advantages of mind control is in its effectiveness, power, and strength. Mind control is the best method of initiating a change of thoughts in another person. You could argue and debate with someone the whole day, but it might not alter their opinions. People tend to be a lot more irrational than they might care to agree and, in several cases, have a psychological immunity towards reasonable thinking and facts. Moreover, emotions play a more important role than rational and intelligent thinking. People tend to make decisions based on their emotions and then try to justify them by using rational thinking. Mind control allows you to appeal to their minds as well as their hearts. Instead of trying to steer them towards a specific direction against their will, you can make them want to change their minds.

Some other advantages of mind control are:

- **You will have inner peace** – Mental strength is a feeling of being in control while staying calm and strong.
- **You can be the master of your mind** – When you start practicing gaining control over your thoughts, it will start becoming a part of you, and soon it will become natural. Your subconscious mind will automatically start the positive distraction when you need to fight off negativity.
- **You will face less conflict** – You will feel less irritated when negative thoughts don't consume your mind. When you feel calmer, you gain the ability to disengage yourself from any conflict.

Chapter 9: Dark Games People Use to Manipulate You

There are several mental games that manipulators play in order to get what they want. One of the most core aspects of being human is that every one of us has made up our minds regarding someone's behavior or intentions. In simpler terms, we all make assumptions. And these assumptions are not always backed up by evidence. People become more and more suspicious the moment they think that they are being manipulated. Most of the time, the actions that people take arise out of ego despite the agendas on their minds. Mind games are something that is carefully designed to get the desired outcome, and it involves a series of recurring actions. There is always gimmick associated with them, or they have a hidden agenda.

Mind games are sometimes also used in hypnotism because they help in making suggestions. As you have already seen in the previous chapters, hypnotism is all about giving suggestions. But sometimes, these suggestions are not as effective as you want them to be, and in that case, people turn to dark games because victims often do not even realize that they are being subjected to some type of dark mind game. And then, there are also situations where mind games are used by manipulators just because they are seeking amusement or pleasure. One of the reasons why mind games are so popular is that they are very effective when it comes to diminishing the psychological strength and assured feeling that the victim has. The victim starts entering a zone where he/she thinks that they do not have any control whatsoever on their thoughts or actions. And so, when manipulators use these mind games on their victims, they can successfully satisfy their twisted desires.

In fact, manipulators who use dark mind games on their victims refrain from seeing them as humans. They rather treat their victims as toys, and so they keep playing them until they are happy. There are also certain manipulators to whom the only known means of manipulation is playing dark games, and these manipulators can be quite dangerous indeed.

In this chapter, we are going to talk about different types of dark mind games that people use to manipulate others.

Ultimatum

One of the worst types of manipulative techniques is ultimatums. These are basically final conditions or propositions and can be used in different perspectives. The manipulator puts a choice in front of the victim, and this choice is usually a very severe one. But not all ultimatums are mind games. Some factors should be considered before classifying an ultimatum as a dark game, and these are –

- Nature of the choice or ultimatum put forward by the person
- The intention of the person behind giving the ultimatum
- The relationship between the person giving the ultimatum and the victim
- The type of person who is giving this ultimatum

An ultimatum will not be considered as a dark mind game or a tool of manipulation if the person who is giving it genuinely wants your good and well-being, and there is a solid reason behind that ultimatum. For example, if your parents or spouse gives you an ultimatum where they actually have your well-being in mind, it won't be a dark ultimatum. But if there are any dark intentions involved, you need to be very careful about those. If the person is giving you an ultimatum because he/she wants you to leave a bad habit, say smoking, then it is not an ultimatum.

An ultimatum can be classified as dark when the choice requires you to do something that you won't do under normal circumstances, and it involves you going against your moral standards. Such dark games are used by manipulators because they want to test how far the victim is ready to go for them and how much they are willing to compromise. Now, the person who is giving you this ultimatum is usually a person who is close to you. It can be a sibling, a parent, your spouse, or even a colleague. In extreme cases, the ultimatums given by the manipulator can also be harmful to you. In fact, there have also been situations where the victim couldn't put up with those ultimatums and ended up taking his/her own life.

Ultimatums are often found in toxic relationships. If your partner ever says things that begin like this – 'If you truly love me like you say you do, you will...' No matter what follows this particular framing of words, it is not healthy, and it is a toxic mind game. But when this happens, the only way out is to tell yourself that it is you who is in control of yourself. And this line of talk is not related to love at all. Loving your partner doesn't mean doing everything they ask you to do. It means loving your partner but not agree to any request that makes you feel uncomfortable. The fact that your partner is using this phrase means that they are using manipulation to get things their way.

Playing Hard to Get

This is another very commonly used dark mind game, and the worst part is that in our culture, this tactic is often passed off as being normal. In this tactic, people do not agree to requests or deny going on a date just because they want to increase your desire for them. The risky nature of this manipulation tactic lies in the fact that the manipulator uses it once he/she has build a bond with you. So, imagine the situation when things are all well, and you both are happy, and suddenly your partner starts ghosting you and denies your requests. They are playing hard to get once you have become closely attached to them. The moment one partner becomes reliant on the other, that is when the person starts distancing themselves to create this dark mind game. This is not healthy at all. In such a case, the victim starts feeling neglected, and they start doing whatever they can to win back the attention. This same pattern continues for a while, after which the manipulator automatically gets the upper hand in the equation. This power is what manipulators seek so that they can use it to fulfill their hidden motives, and the victim becomes unstable and confused.

Some other things that you will notice in people who are trying to play hard to get are as follows –

- They give attention at one moment and then disappear the next. Suppose they might be flirting with you now, but tomorrow, they might not reply to any of your texts.
- Withholding sex and, at the same time, exposing you to limited physical contact is also a way of playing hard to get. In some cases, the manipulator also puts up a show of accidental physical contact.
- They act non-responsive to whatever you say or do and show that they do not have any interest in you whatsoever.
- They are friendly, but they also indulge in sarcastic comments from time to time. They taunt you and tease you.
- If you are in a relationship with the manipulator, then you will often notice them talking to other people and not you. They may even date other people or flirt with them.
- They start prioritizing other things and act as if they are busy all the time.

Implied Breakup

Another form of emotional blackmail through dark games is using an implied breakup. In these cases, the manipulator might tell you that they want to break up with you, but their actual intention is not the breakup. Instead, they want to see how you react to the breakup. In their deepest mind, they hope that you will be overcome by pain and grief, and then finally, agree to whatever they want and cater to their emotional needs. This can be called as one of the extreme steps of emotional manipulation, and yet it is one of the most popular dark games.

Sometimes, the break up might not even be a direct one. The manipulator might make you feel it by giving you occasional hints. All of this immediately gives rise to the birth of doubt in the mind of the victim. Some simple gestures can make this happen, for example, making future plans and yet excluding the partner from it. They might even say things like – 'Don't bother yourself so much because it's only a matter of a few days, and after that, I'll leave.' So, what they are trying to do here is giving their partner a hint that a breakup is possible in the future.

Since a lack of security in the relationship creeps in, the victim is afraid of losing his/her love, and so the manipulator gets the upper hand in the relationship. They might even take extreme steps to achieve it. For example, they might pack their bags and attempt to leave, but the moment the victim breaks down and becomes sad, the manipulator turns back and stays, but that moment immediately gives him/her full control of the partner. In this process, the manipulator paints his/her image as the generous one in the relationship.

So, these were some of the typical dark games that you should be aware of.

Chapter 10: How to Make People Obey Your Commands Through Mind Control Techniques?

In this book, we have already discussed the topic of psychological manipulation in almost all aspects of life, and now it's time that I talk about a few mind control techniques. These techniques are quite easy, and they function mostly by pressing some emotional hot buttons of the person. The ultimate result is that upon using these techniques, people will start obeying your commands. Now, when we talk about mind control in this perspective, we do not mean that people will do whatever you ask them to do. It is more about influencing someone's actions.

<u>*Gaslighting*</u>

The first technique that we are going to talk about is gaslighting, and it is one of the most popularly used techniques indeed. This is a term that we all have heard at one point or the other. But can you define it, or can you point out as to what it really is? Like every other subject, knowledge is power even in dark psychology, and so, if you know about gaslighting, not only can you protect yourself from it but also use it to your benefit in order to make people obey you. It is, in fact, a very covert technique, and thus, it is not easy to spot it at once. Gaslighting is such an effective technique that it is also used in interrogations. The main goal of this technique is to use information in such a way that the person is no longer able to trust their own instinct or judgment, and they are totally confused. They become anxious and start relying on you for everything. That is when they will take all your suggestions and do whatever you want them to do.

The mental equilibrium of a person is targeted in a very specific manner in gaslighting. Also, everything happens in a systematic process. The self-esteem and self-confidence of the person also take a hit. If the person used to be independent before then now, they will no longer be able to do things on their own and depend on you for making decisions. In short, you get full control over the person.

One of the advantages of using gaslighting to make people do what you want is that people don't recognize that you are gaslighting them. When used effectively, you can actually trigger the stress response in that person, which means that after a certain point of time, the person will completely surrender to you.

So, if a person has been trying to communicate for a long time and you have been putting them off, then there will come the point when they'll become frustrated. And if you keep doing this over and over again, it is in the tendency of a human body to trigger the survival system of the body. When that happens, a person is not able to make sense of things the way he/she used to, and their mind is clouded with everything. Thus, helplessness starts setting in as an automatic and adaptive response. Thinking too much at that moment becomes difficult for the person, and so he/she chooses the comfort zone over everything else. They no longer try to stand up for anything and happily choose what is given to them. So, things like reward and punishment, illusions and lies, and fear tactics are used cunningly to make others obey commands. If you are trying to maintain your superiority, then this technique is definitely going to be a lot helpful.

But, if we are to think of the contrary, and suppose you are being the subject of gaslighting from someone else, then here are some tips that you should keep in mind –

- No matter what, you have to try and step outside of the bubble that you are in. I know that this is easier said than done, but no matter how hard you feel it is, do not give up. You should also try to figure out why someone is trying to gaslight you in the first place. Is it related to work, or does it have anything to do with your love life?
- Remind yourself that if someone is trying to gaslight you, it is usually not about you. It is about the manipulator and their need to have power over you. That person is flawed and feels insecure in the position they are currently in, and so they are trying to intimidate you through gaslighting. It is true that it is next to impossible for you to understand the motives or characters of the gaslighter, and so, you also have to make yourself understand that you cannot do anything about his condition.

- You need to distance yourself from the person who is gaslighting you. Don't be as easy going and readily available as you used to be. Remind yourself that it is your self-esteem that is being compromised, and is any relationship worth taking all that trouble?
- Another advice that I can give you is that don't try to confront the person who is gaslighting you. They do not usually take confrontations healthily, and you will be the one who'll be hurt by the process. Gaslighters tend to get defensive and will try every means necessary to undermine you during the confrontation.

Fear of Alienation

The next mind control method that we are going to talk about is the fear of alienation. In this technique, the manipulator has to befriend someone at first. After that, you have to keep on developing this bond up to a point, after which the person feels that this relationship is the most precious one they have. In simpler words, the victim then won't be able to live without the manipulator because he/she thinks that they don't have anyone else in the world who can provide them with such a bonding. They feel that the bonding they hold with the manipulator is the most priceless thing in their lives, and thus, they cannot afford to lose it.

But once that dependency is established, the manipulator can exercise full control over the victim because he/she fears alienation. Even if the victim doesn't realize it, the manipulator can remind them that in the outside world, no one else can provide them with such a meaningful bond. It doesn't matter if they don't seem to be totally convinced at the moment because later on, they will realize themselves how lonely the outside world is. The fear of alienation will start kicking in, and that's when the person will obey the commands of the manipulator.

Repetition

Repetition is actually a very powerful tool and has immense effects on persuasion. One of the greatest tools in persuasive techniques is repetition, and it is not only effective in the verbal form but also in the written form. A repetition strategy that has been planned and executed in the perfect way will definitely help to put forth your message in a much better and effective way. There have been several psychological studies on the use of repetition as a persuasive strategy. These studies have shown how repeating something can change how a person perceives a certain subject. It also leaves a positive influence as far as agreeing with the message is concerned.

Frequent repetition can also make others believe in things that are not even true. This is mainly because people don't have the capability to distinguish between the truth and familiarity. If we are to put this in simpler words, I would say that the human brain loves to accept facts that are put forward. It doesn't love to do the legwork, and in that way, you can call the brain lazy. It is because of this habit that there is a tendency in the human brain to choose a way that involves the least amount of resistance. This trait is very deep-seated in all of us throughout evolution. When your brain is exposed to information that it has encountered in the past, then it seems familiar to the brain, and it also becomes easier to process that information. So, when the mind comes face to face with a repetitive fact, it likes that fact more, and so, a bias works here to make the person feel that just because the information has been repeated, it is true.

This also happens in relationships. Think about how you start liking someone more when you start seeing them more often. It happens because your brain is becoming familiar with that face and so urging you to like that person. I am not saying that is how people fall in love, but of course, as far as the formation of a bond in the initial days is concerned, this is how it works. This is also how all of these things happen – going to the same cafes and restaurants, hanging out with the same friends, going for a run on the same trail, and ordering the same food.

There is another thing to keep in mind with respect to repetition. It is a very effective strategy, especially when the audience you are talking to you is not too much attentive to what you are saying. But for repetition to be actually effective, you should refrain from overdoing it. Many people think that the more you repeat, the more effective it becomes. But it is quite the opposite because after a certain point of time, repeating something has the opposite effect on the person because he/she then becomes irritated. One of the most common examples where repetition is actively used as a tactic to persuade people is when politicians use repetition in their speech to make people believe whatever they are saying.

Think about it this way – when you listen to something for the first time, do you believe it right away? No, right? It can be because of several reasons. You might not be able to see what value it has at that moment, or it might simply not resonate with you. Moreover, when you already have too much on your plate, something new would only make matters worse. So, the most common response people have when you ask them something new is that they don't have enough time for it. In short, the answer will be no. When fear is involved, it would be quite difficult for you to change that decision. But when the subject has been said before, it is no longer something new, and the person feels familiar to the subject. Then, it becomes easier to make them agree to it.

Flattery

The next thing that you can use to control someone's mind is flattery or compliments. There are so many benefits associated with using flattery in a conversation and all of these things point to one end result – taking the upper hand and making someone obey your commands. If you want to switch the focus of the conversation to something speicifc that you have in mind, flattery has been proven to be the way out. Think about anything you want to compliment the person on – it can be their outfit, their hair, the way they talk, or anything. The moment you give a compliment, all the attention will be drawn to that and you will have the perfect chance to change the narration to something that you want to discuss.

Another way in which flattery can prove to be of great help is when you are trying to demand attention to yourself. You can simply go and tell the person that you understand them and listening to others is a skill that you hold dear. Flattery will also help you strengthen the bond that you have with that other person. Let us say that you are in a social setting and you want the other person to think that you both make a good match because you flatter each other. This should make the othe person look at you with friendship.

Guilt-Tripping

One of the most powerful emotions that you can use against another person is guilt. But I must warn you that if you want to wield the power of guilt into persuading someone to make some decisions, then you also have to tread extremely carefully. Guilt-tripping, when gone wrong, can even give rise to anger, and things will not go as you planned. So, you have to take every step necessary to ensure that your plan does not backfire at you.

If you want someone to admit something that they don't want to, don't go and accuse them straightaway. That is only going to steer them away. But if you start asking the right questions that will lead you to the desired conclusion, then you might be able to get what you want. And even if nothing works, asking a lot of questions often helps you to catch someone in the middle of a lie, and then you can use it against them.

Another very important aspect of guilt-tripping is that you have to actively play the victim; otherwise, the person will not feel guilty at all. You have to paint a picture of their character that says that they are habitually into a series of things that keep repeating. You also have to make them feel that you don't deserve to be treated in that way. Let us say that you want the person to admit to things that you didn't like. Then, you have to bring up certain similar things that the person did in the past. This has a high chance of making them feel guilty even more than before.

You can also say things like – 'I am starting to question our equation since you did that thing.' But whatever you do, the ultimate aim has to be that the person should feel it inside them that they have to do everything to prove themselves to you. You can also try another tactic, and that is, you can remind them of all the favors and good things that you have pulled off for them. It will help you even more if the gesture you are talking about is a grand one or something big that you did for them.

You will also notice that when you are trying to guilt-trip someone else, they will make attempts to make it all about you. I will advise you to be aware of that because even if you have not done anything, they will try to pin everything on you. Your task is to not acknowledge anything even if you have done it and reverse all the blame towards the person. Even if the situation comes to a point where you are angry, but you don't know how to let it out, you can say things like – if only you hadn't made me feel like this, I wouldn't have yelled at you. The ultimate aim should be guilt-tripping the person for everything you can think of.

Sarcasm

Persuading someone to do something or making them obey your commands needs you to develop a strong voice, and that can be done through sarcasm. But you also need to use sarcasm properly. What is the main idea behind the different techniques of mind control? They are aimed at making the other person think about your point and then accept your opinion. And, sarcasm can do that.

Now, as you probably already know, a strongly negative remark can be made through sarcasm, and you can even show your anger towards other's opinions. If someone is making an opinion that you don't like, then you can mock their point of view through sarcasm. Sarcasm can also be created by posing questions that have implied answers. Another common way of creating sarcasm is by making fun of other's opinions by cracking jokes.

If you are not a sarcastic person by nature, then developing that tone can be a bit intimidating in the beginning, but with time, you will be able to master it.

Diversion

This is a bit advanced mind control technique to persuade someone. Also, this technique is slightly towards the ethical side and is also less aggressive in nature. The main motive of using diversion is to make the person not notice the part of the story that you want to hide from them. So, if the conversation is going towards a direction that you don't want, then you can quickly divert the topic in a different direction.

So, these were some of the ways in which mind control can be used to get what you want. But there are some techniques which work only after the other person has shown you some form of resistance. Let us say you want to try out a new restaurant in town and your friend is saying no to it. How will you make him agree? You can frame your sentence like this - 'So, are you not willing to try these new dishes?' I am sure the reaction to this question will be in your favor. Whenever the word 'willing' is used in sentences like these, people's responses to your questions and requests automatically change. Ultimately, the question might seem that you are asking your friend about his/her preference in food, but the hidden motive is questioning their character as to what kind of person they are not to try new food.

One thing that is common in most mind control techniques is that they make everything personal. People tend to respond better when things are personal. You should also think about what the other person will stand to gain from the arrangement you have in mind. I know that you might think it's not a big difference to you, but it is to the other person. Whenever the person has some kind of gain from the request, it is easier to persuade them. So, they will not feel like they are losing anything by saying yes to you. In fact, they will stand to gain something.

Chapter 11: Warning Signs of Manipulation in Relationships

Just because you are in love with someone doesn't mean that you are not being manipulated by that person. In fact, the trickiest thing about identifying manipulation in relationships is that it is very hard to notice. People are so blinded by love that they deny seeing the bad in others, and they can't seem to identify that they are being manipulated. When you are in a relationship with someone who is manipulative, they always put their own needs first and so they twist your desires, thoughts, wants, and actions in a way that will help them fulfill their motives. I know that all of this sounds quite scary, but if you want to ensure that it doesn't happen to you, there are some warning signs that you should look out for.

Also, if you have started dating the person only recently, identifying these signs can be difficult – even more, when things seem to be going pretty well on the surface. Everyone wants their relationship to be like fairy tales in books. And, when things don't go as planned, it's natural for a person to be in denial. But you will have to accept at one point that your relationship does have the signs of manipulation that we are about to discuss in this chapter.

Your Partner Makes You Feel as If It Is Always Your Fault

Guilt is where all the manipulation. Most of the time, you will see that even when you are not at fault, your partner will try to make you feel that everything happened because of you or something that you did. The manipulating partner knows that if you start feeling guilty, it would be easier to make you do things that your partner wants. Let me give you an example so that you can understand this better – Sarah has cooked dinner for Nate, and when Sarah asks Nate whether he liked the dinner or not, his reply was somewhat like this: 'It was alright since it was not what I thought you'd make but anyways, I am happy as long as you are happy and I don't care if it means that I have to set aside my wishes.' So, do you see how Nate totally turned the sentence and made it about Sarah? Sarah might think that Nate is simply a caring and loving partner, but he is only guilt-tripping her, and that is, in no sense, even close to what love is.

Another characteristic feature of a partner being manipulative in a relationship is that they will try to portray that you are not good at loving someone and that they are doing a better job than you when it comes to maintaining the relationship. This is quite sick because then the other partner feels that they have to set aside all their wishes, aspirations, and priorities only because they need to show how much they love him/her.

Your Partner Always Over-Delivers

People often don't understand that over-delivering is indeed one of the toxic traits that you must be aware of in a relationship. This is when the manipulative partner is going to bomb you with thousands of compliments, gifts, love, and so on – basically anything and everything that you desire, and this will make you feel that your partner is doing things for you that no one would ever do. These situations might even feel like a dream come true because you don't have to do anything, and yet your partner will keep showering you with everything good. But when too many good things happen too early in a relationship, that is when you need to be careful because this is not healthy.

These manipulative partners want to give you everything so that you think they are perfect and irresistible. You might even think that your partner is like no one you have ever met, but that's just it – they are putting on a façade, and that's not going to last forever. They are hiding their true selves from you. I am not saying that you should be suspicious of anyone who is good to you, but if someone over delivers love and kindness, then that is toxic. When someone is over-delivering, they push the relationship, and it starts moving faster than it should, and soon, the manipulative partner takes the upper hand and gains control of the relationship.

Your Partner Forces His/Her Insecurities On You

This is another common trait that you should look out for in relationships. They are so controlling and want to have the upper hand on your reactions toward them that they are even ready to force their own insecurities on you. For example, if your partner has been cheated multiple times before and asks you not to have friends of the opposite sex so that they can be at peace, then this kind of behavior is not healthy. Any relationship should not be defined by the insecurities or struggles of one partner.

The moment someone points out their mistakes, the manipulators often come up with excuses like this – 'I only acted this way because I didn't want to lose you and I was scared.' But this is no excuse for bad behavior, and the only motive behind this excuse is that the focus of the conversation is removed from what you wanted to say. When someone is manipulating you into feeling whatever they are feeling, then that is quite different from someone who actually cares about your feelings. It is guilt that drives manipulation, whereas love is portrayed through consideration.

Your Partner Does Not Communicate Clearly

Sketchy communication is one of the biggest red flags that you should be aware of. A healthy relationship is built on communication, and if it is absent, there are a lot of things that could go wrong. For example, your partner might have promised you that you two would go out for a movie together, and just when you got ready, he/she calls you with an excuse that they won't be able to make it. Wheneever it comes to making commitments, they fail horribly, and so no matter how many promises they make, their actions are never able to prove you that they are indeed going to keep the promise.

So, if your partner has been displaying this sort of behavior for quite some time, you shouldn't be the victim of it. You should be with someone who has it in them to follow through with the promises and commitments they make.

They Do Not Like Your Independent Nature

Manipulators often do not like it when their partners are self-empowered and independent, and this is mainly because they can be manipulative as long as they are in control. But when someone is independent, it is difficult to manipulate them. If your partner truly loves you, then they will never stop you from being your true self. In fact, they will encourage you to be more independent.

For example, if your partner tries to guilt-trip you every time you want to spend time with your family or friends, then they are manipulative. Being in a relationship doesn't mean forgetting your individual self. Even when you are with someone, you still have your own life, which needs to be maintained.

So, if you want to test whether your partner is manipulative or not – make some decisions for yourself from time to time and see whether your partner supports you or not. Most importantly, make decisions that are regarding issues that do not include your partner, and if your partner is still with you on that decision, then they are not toxic.

They Make You Feel Responsible For Everything Including Their Own Emotions

Another very predominant characteristic of manipulators is that they do not have any sense of accountability, and so, you will often find them making you feel guilty and responsible for something they are feeling. For example, if your partner is not happy with something, they might make you feel that it has to do with you. If your partner is angry, they might portray it that their anger roots from something you did. They will try to make you feel that your life is not under your control and that everything that happens around you is because of something you did. This is totally insane!

They Often Use Negative Humor in Conversations

We all have encountered people who use negative humor to make us feel small and insulted. But what if it is your partner who does that? Just because he/she is your partner, you should not give them a free pass to commit any mistake they want. If they are making any critical remark that makes you unhappy, you have to say it out loud. These remarks are often veiled with humor or sarcasm and the result is that you feel insecure and small.

The comments can be about anything – about your credentials, your background, your professional life, or even your appearance. It can be about something as small as the brand of the mobile phone you use. They simply want to establish their superiority by making you feel bad for being you.

So, when you are in a relationship, figure these things out with time. There is no rush, and the best way to do it is to take things slow and get to know the person properly.

Chapter 12: How to Avoid Being Manipulated?

Many people use manipulation to accomplish their own ends. It is very important that you prevent yourself from getting manipulated; otherwise, you can end up doing something that will harm you. In order to avoid being manipulated, first, you need to understand that someone is trying to manipulate you, and then you need to prevent yourself from being intimidated by it.

Let us quickly go over some of the signs that will help you whether or not someone is trying to manipulate you.

- The most common trick that is used by the manipulators is an exaggeration. In this case, you can either tell them to stop directly or you can go for an indirect approach. Focus on the facts, and ask them informative questions.
- Manipulators feed on your fears. This is another common tactic used by them. They will try to scare you in order to make you agree to their point. The things they say may

instigate threats of backlash or physical harm or fear of monetary losses or rejection. In situations like this, don't use direct methods to counteract. Instead, use tactics to end the conversation or move to a more crowded place while having this conversation.

- Some manipulators try to establish control over you and the current situation by constantly giving you reminders about their own powers and importance. This makes them dominant and puts the other person in a situation of disadvantage. You can stop this by doing the same, i.e., reminding them of your importance and powers so that there is balance in the playing field.

- Most of the time, manipulators know that their arguments are mainly based on lies, half-truths, or shaky logic. So they try to portray themselves as an expert. In situations like this, they often talk in monologues and at high speed so that you don't get any time to point out the flaws and deception. In situations like these, you can tell them to slow down and repeat their point because in order to give you a better understanding of the thing they want to say to you.

When you suspect that you are being manipulated, ask yourselves a few questions like "what is the motive of the person?" or "who gets benefited by it?" or "who is being exploited?" or "who is at a disadvantage?" etc. If you get uncertain or negative answers, either way, it can mean that you are facing a manipulator. You can prevent these situations by giving well-considered responses, being aware, or you can also utilize your assertive communication skills when required. You can also directly say "no" to that person but think nicely before doing so because this kind of assertiveness can bring in negative repercussions. In case you are not comfortable with direct approaches, talk to someone trustworthy, and seek their opinion and advice in this matter. In extreme situations, you can try contacting the necessary authorities, who can help you in figuring out what to do and how you can proceed.

There are several ways to avoid being manipulated. Let us see some of those.

<u>Have Knowledge about Your Own Fundamental Human Rights</u>

Always be aware of your fundamental rights while dealing with a person who is psychologically manipulative. This is important so that you can understand whether your rights are being violated or not. You have all the rights to take your own stand and defend your own rights as long as you mean no harm to others. On the other hand, if you harm others, then you may be deprived of these rights. Let us see some of the fundamental rights that you always need to keep in mind:

- The right to get treated with respect
- The right to build your own healthy and happy life
- The right to care for yourself and protect yourself from emotional, mental, or physical threats
- The right to have opinions which are not similar to that of the others
- The right to get what you deserve or the thing you paid for
- The right to say "no" without a feeling of guilt
- The right to prioritize things
- The right to express your wants, opinions, and feelings

These rights are your boundaries that need to be protected. However, these rights are very much prone to get violated by people who do not give much respect to these rights. Psychological manipulators will desperately try to deprive you of your rights so that they can take advantage of you and can take control of the situation. Always remember that you have the moral authority and power to declare that you are the person who can take charge of your life and not the manipulator.

Stay Distant

An effective way of identifying a manipulator is by keeping a watch of their behaviors in different situations and in front of different people. All of us have a slight degree of social differentiation, but psychological manipulators have extreme degrees of social differentiation. They can be extremely rude to certain individuals while being extra polite to a few. At one moment, they can be fiercely aggressive while being totally helpless at the next moment. If you notice these behavioral traits in an individual, then try to maintain a safe distance from them.

Try to avoid getting engaged in conversations with them unless there is an absolute necessity to do so. The reasons for psychological manipulation are deep-seated and complex, and it is absolutely not your job to save or change them.

Avoid Self-blame and Personalization

Always keep in mind that the manipulator's agenda is to find your weaknesses and exploit them. In situations like these, it is very likely of you to blame yourself for not being able to satisfy the manipulator. So, it is very important that you constantly remind yourself that you are not the problem here, and it is the manipulator who is making you feel like this so that they can exploit you. Ask yourself questions like "Am I being treated with respect?" or "Are these demands reasonable?" or "Will I be benefited?" etc. Questions like these will make you understand the reality of the situation and help you act accordingly.

Ask Them Probing Questions and Keep the Focus on Them

It is very likely that the manipulators are going to make certain demands or requests to you. You'll tend to feel an urge to go out of your way to meet their needs. In these situations, try to put your focus on the manipulator and ask them probing questions to check whether that person is aware of their scheme's inequity. You should ask them questions like "Do you think it is fair?" or "How is this reasonable?". When you do this, the manipulator gets a taste of his ploy. If that person has a bit of self-awareness, he will back down immediately. In case the manipulator disregards your questions, and continue making unjust demands, try and impose power on the conversation and stop it.

Make Use of Time at Your Advantage

For maximizing their pressure and control over you, it is likely for the manipulator to ask answers from you immediately. In situations like these, don't respond right away. Instead, try to leverage your time and distance yourself from their immediate influence. Responses like "I'll get back to you" or "I need some time" are perfect in these situations. Take time and evaluate all the pros and cons and then make a decision.

Learn to Say "No" Firmly and Diplomatically

The ability to say "no" to a person diplomatically while being firm is an art of communication. It allows you to take your own stand and also helps you to maintain a workable relationship. Always remind yourself that saying "no" is your fundamental right, and you are able to do it wherever and whenever you feel the need to do it without feeling bad or guilty. Set your priorities and take charge of your life.

Set the Consequence

When a manipulator forces you to push your boundaries and violate your rights, they are likely to not accept "no" for an answer. So, employ the consequences. The ability to identify and assert the consequences is a very effective skill that you can use to shut a difficult person. It makes the manipulator stop and forces him or her to treat you with respect rather than violating your rights.

Safely Confront Bullies

A psychological manipulator turns into a bully when that person tries to bring harm to you. Always keep in mind that bullies always exploit those whom they consider are weaker than them. So if you continue to stay compliant and passive, you are more likely to be on their target list. Most of the bullies are cowards from the inside, and so they stop when their targets start showing backbone. If the targets start to give them direct responses or take their own stand, then the bullies are likely to back off. It is effective in all situations like office environments, domestic environments, and even in schoolyards.

Chapter 13: How to Analyze People?

Is it hard for you to understand why people do the things that they do? Do you need some help when it's about romance? Do you need to improve your people skills? Do you want to succeed at work? Is it hard for you to understand what your kids are thinking? This blog can definitely help you, no matter why you want to learn how to analyze people.

Logic alone cannot help you if you want to understand an individual. In order to understand how to analyze the non-verbal initiative cues that are given off by people, you have to give in to the other important forms of information. In order to do this, you have to give up any emotional baggage or preconceptions like ego clashes or old resentments that might be stopping you from clearly seeing someone—the clue to this to receive information in a neutral manner without contorting it and staying objective.

Whether you are trying to read your kids, your partner, co-worker, or boss, in order to do so accurately, you have to bring down some walls and surrender to any biases. You have to willingly let go of old ideas that can be very limiting. Those who are able to analyze other people properly are trained to read and analyze the invisible. They have learned to look further than where people generally look by utilizing their "super senses" and are able to access life-changing intuitive insights.

Analyzing People Effectively

In order to recognize how your mannerisms and actions can affect other people, you have to be able to understand the differences between how you communicate with different people and how you act around them. Some notable people in your life could be any of the following:

- Your closest friend
- Someone with whom you don't click

- Your parents
- A professor with whom you struggled the most
- Your boss
- Your children, if applicable
- Your significant other

You need to take note of how the different behavior of all these people affects you and how your actions make you appear to them. A good method of practicing this is by thinking about how other people might behave around you based on how they consider you in their lives. Maybe they act in a different way around you than they do around other people.

People You Do Know vs. People You Don't

How you see and behave towards someone is greatly affected by how well you know them or how well you want to know them. Your closeness to someone or distance from someone in the aspect of your relationships will define the things you need to think about when you are analyzing both your and the other person's behavior while you are interacting with them. In the end, this will also help you determine how you want to make use of these insights in order to correctly analyze what they are trying to communicate with you.

Here are four examples to better elaborate on this concept:

1. You have an unstable relationship with your mother. Your relationship is long-term and intensely involved. Your aim is to try to find out what the origin of the complication was and fix your relationship with her. To do this, you first need to consider a few things: how she fulfills her needs, her points of concentration, comprehensive information about her personal life, the way she communicates with you, her impulses, preferences, and her body language. The most important thing that you need to figure out is her motivation.
2. You have been in a relationship with your significant other for about a year. As its starting to get more serious, you are considering asking him/her to move in with you. The relationship is intimate and medium-term. Your first objective should be to consider whether moving in together would be a smart move. You want to figure out how they might respond when you ask them the question. The important factors that you need to consider are their past experiences and personal life, how they communicate with you, their impulses, preferences, and

body language. In addition to that, you also need to consider how they go about fulfilling their requirements, their points of concentration, and their drive. You can also acquire more insight by consulting family and friends.

3. You are thinking about sharing innovation for a business idea with a co-worker. You have a relatively superficial relationship with this co-worker, and it is medium-term. You want to observe their behavior to determine whether the two of you are compatible to work together and whether he or she would be a suitable business partner before expressing your idea. You want to figure out how you should approach them to get the best response. You need to observe the following factors: how they verbally communicate with you, their impulses, preferences, and their body language. In addition to that, defining their points of concentration and rive, along with having some insight into their past experiences and personal life, could also be very helpful in this case.

4. In the initial process of meeting someone, you might ask yourself whether they are attracted to you. You are attracted to them; however, before expressing your feelings to

them, you want to get to know them better. At this time, your interpersonal relationship with this other person is superficial and quite new. In addition to that, before expressing your feelings, you want to be sure that you are correctly interpreting their signals in case the feelings are not mutual. You need to pay attention to a few things with your first encounters with this person. Some of the factors you need to consider are their preferences, how they speak with you, their body language, and how they carry themselves around you. You can subtly acquire some details like their previous history with relationships in your first few conversations and use that information to determine how you will act.

In all the above examples, some of the main things that you should take into account are the insight and information you have on them, their motivation, and the extent of your relationship with them. These three factors will help you determine how to make use of the acquired information.

Techniques By Which You Can Analyze People

Sense emotional energy

The energy or "vibe" we give off is well expressed by our emotions. Our intuition helps us register these. Some people help improve our vitality and mood, and it feels good to be around them. However, others can be draining, and you just want to move away from them. Even though this subtle energy is invisible, it can be felt feet or inches from the body. It is known as chi in Chinese medicine. It's a vitality that is important to health.

Methods to analyze emotional energy:

1. Notice their laugh and tone of voice – A lot about our state of emotions can be conveyed via the volume and tone of our voice. Vibrations are created by the frequencies of sounds. Try to notice how the tone of someone's voice affects you while you are trying to analyze them. Ask yourself whether their tone feels whiny, snippy, abrasive, or soothing.
2. Notice the feel of their touch, hug, and a handshake – much like an electric current, emotional energy is also shared through physical contact. Ask yourself whether a

hug or a handshake feels confident, comfortable, warm, or off-putting. Is the other person's hand limp, indicating that they are timid and non-committal? Or are they clammy, indicating anxiety?

3. Notice people's eyes – People's eyes send powerful energy. Studies have revealed that similar to the brain that sends electromagnetic signals beyond the body, and the eyes do this as well. Take time and try to watch people's eyes. Are they angry? Mean? Tranquil? Sexy? Caring? Also, try to understand whether someone seems to be hiding or guarding something, or are they at home in their eyes, which reveals their capability for intimacy.

4. Sense their presence – Someone's presence is like an emotional atmosphere that surrounds us like the sun or a rain cloud. It's not essentially congruent with behavior or words but is the overall energy that is emitted by us. While you are trying to analyze people, try to notice: Are you feeling scared, which is making you want to back off? Or are you attracted by their friendly presence?

Listen to your intuition

Intuition is not what your head says. It's what your gut feels. It is the non-verbal information you can perceive beyond logic, words, and body language. What counts the most when you want to understand someone is who the person is from within and not just their outer appearance. With the help of intuition, you can reveal a richer story by seeing further than the obvious.

Some intuitive cues you can look into:

1. Look out for intuitive empathy – You can experience an intense form of empathy when you can feel people's emotions and symptoms in your body. Therefore, when you are analyzing people, try to notice whether you are upset or depressed after an uneventful meeting or if your back hurts suddenly. Get some feedback to determine whether this is empathy or not.
2. Watch out for flashes of insight – You might get an "ah-ha" about people while you are conversing about them. It might come in a flash so stay alert. If not, you might miss out on it. These critical insights might get lost as we tend to move onto the next thought very fast.

3. Feel the goosebumps – Goosebumps are amazing intuitive signals that tell us when we resonate with people who are saying something that we connect with or when they inspire or move us. It can also take place when you feel a sense of déjà-vu. Déjà-vu is a feeling of recognition that you might have known someone before, although you haven't actually met.
4. Honor your gut feelings – During your first meetings, try to listen to your gut. Before you even have an opportunity to ponder about it, a visceral reaction already takes place. It conveys whether you are relaxed or not. Gut feelings take place very fast as a primal response. They act as your internal truth meter and convey to you whether you can trust someone or not.

Observe body language cues

According to studies, words account for only seven percent of our method of communication. The remaining is represented by the tone of our voice (thirty percent) and body language (fifty-five percent). Stay fluid and relaxed while reading body language cues. Don't get overly analytical or intense. Simple sit back, be comfortable, and observe.

1. Interpret facial expression – Our feelings and emotions tend to get stamped on our faces. Over-thinking or worry is conveyed by the deep frown lines. The smile lines of joy are depicted by the crow's feet. Bitterness, contempt, or anger is signaled by pursed lips. Grinding teeth or clenched jaw are signs of tension.
2. Pay attention to posture – When you are trying to analyze someone's posture, ask yourself: Is their chest puffed out when they are walking, which is a sign of a big ego? Or do they cower while walking, which is a sign of low self-esteem? Or, is their head held high, confident?
3. Notice their appearance – When you are analyzing others, pay attention to their appearance. Are they wearing a t-shirt and jeans, indicating that they are dressed casually for comfort? A power suit with properly shined shoes, indicating ambition and being dressed for success? A pendant like a Buddha or a cross indicating their spiritual values? A well-fitted top with cleavage, indicating a seductive choice?

Learning how to analyze other people accurately takes time and practice, and obviously, every rule has some exceptions. However, you can improve your abilities to analyze others, communicate properly with them, and understand their thinking by keeping these points in mind while building your powers of observation.

Chapter 14: Psychological Tricks to Examine Human Beings

You must have heard it a lot of times already that communication is the key to everything – be it your personal relationships or your business deals. Everything is carefully balanced on how you choose to communicate with people. But it's easier said than done. It can be really hard to handle people the right way, but there are certain psychological tricks that can come in really handy. They help you to examine the people around you so that you can understand their motives, and they will also make your overall life much easier.

By now, you must have already understood that humans are not at all easy to understand, and they are quite complex. But there are certain patterns in behavior that can be studied to make conclusions. If you think that examining someone can only be done through psychoanalysis and not otherwise, then you are wrong because it can also be done through other tricks, which are relatively easier. In fact, once you finish this chapter, you will realize that nothing is done without reason. Even if a person raises an eyebrow or stands in a particular manner, there is meaning to it, and this meaning, when deciphered, will help you understand that person.

I know what you must be wondering. Telepathy does have a supernatural ring to it, but what we are going to discuss in this book is purely a page from the book of psychology. It is just like any other skill you learn. Understanding and examining a human being is not any different. With time, as you keep practicing, you will notice that you have developed an inner intuition that will always guide you in the right direction. Whether you want to understand how you should approach your boss or in what way you should speak to please your client, all of those tactics can be mastered through some simple psychological tricks. Do you know who the top performers in a company are? They are definitely not the ones who are the smartest in the room. In fact, they are the ones with the best people skills and know how to communicate.

You simply need to practice every day to tune in and understand what every person is thinking or how they are as a person. If you want your relationship-building skills to improve, there are different ways in which you can make educated guesses about people from now on, and we are going to learn them in this chapter.

So, let us have a look at some of these tips and tricks, and I hope you are able to apply them to the person you meet next.

Look Into Their Eyes

I have to say that looking into someone's eyes is the first and foremost trick that everyone should learn. Eyes are the doorway to the mind, and they really convey much more than we can imagine. You will often come in situations where you do not particularly prefer the answer you got, and when that happens, you do not understand why things happened the way they did. You might have expected a different answer, and now that the opposite happened, you can't seem to figure out why. Sounds familiar? Well, then you are in luck here because looking into that person's eyes can get you the answer you are looking for. The first reaction that most people have in such a situation is that they ask the question again, but that is most likely to get you the same answer once again. What you should do is look deep into the eyes of that person and try to understand what you see. When you do that, the person is automatically going to feel as if they are cornered. In short, they will feel a bit of stress, and this stress itself will bring you a lot of answers. Most of the time, in such situations, the person tries to elaborate on why they said what they said.

Apart from the situation I just explained, looking into someone's eyes will help you take a peek into their mind. If someone is trying to dismiss what you are saying or is not liking the conversation, you can make it out if you truly look into their eyes.

Now, let us go into some of the details. One of the first things you should keep in mind is to watch for any changes in the size of the pupil. I am going to give you an example from a study that was published in the year 1965. It was conducted to show the difference in the size of the pupil in response to the information that is given to the people (Eckhard H. Hess, 1965). The psychologists had produced semi-nude pictures belonging to both sexes to female and male participants. There was an increase in the size of the pupils of the female participants when they saw the pictures of men. Similarly, there was an increase in the size of the pupils of the male participants when they saw the pictures of women.

Subsequent studies were done by the same psychologists to find more information. Homosexual participants were included, and the same result was obtained. Their pupils increased in size when they saw pictures of men in semi-nude condition. At the same time, when pictures, where babies were being coddled by mothers were shown to women, their pupils dilated too. So, do you see where this experiment is heading? It is not only arousal that is depicted by the dilation of pupils, but it also shows whether the information shown is interesting and relatable.

Now, let us move on to something much more complex – when you become an expert at reading the eyes, you can also find out whether a person is telling the truth or lying by simply looking at their eyes. In the year 2009, another study was conducted in which one group of participants did not steal, and the other had stoled $20 (Andrea K. Webb, 2009). Whether the participant had stolen the money or not, every one of them were asked to say the same thing that they had not stolen anything. The detection of a thief was possible when pupil dilation was examined with respect to denying the theft. When the pupil dilation of both groups was compared, it was noticed that the ones who were actually lying witnessed an increase in pupil size, which was 1 mm more than those who did not commit the theft.

Another thing about the eyes that you should keep in mind is that when people close their eyes in the middle of a conversation, it is usually because there is some feeling that they are trying hard to bury inside themselves. Or, it can also be that they are trying to hide from the chaos of the outside world. But what you should remember is that closing the eyes does not necessarily mean that the person is afraid of you. In fact, it is quite the opposite. They might be finding you annoying, or something about the conversation is irritating them, which is why they want to shut you out. It makes them feel that even when you are in front of them, closing their eyes means that they can shut you out momentarily and not have to see you.

Find the Hot Buttons

If you want to understand someone and their motives, you have to find out more about their hot buttons. It starts with recognizing the hot buttons first. Hot buttons are people's pain points, and they help you understand what they are thinking. The best way to recognize these points is to ask the right questions. And for that, the first step is to build a rapport and a good bond with the person. In short, you have to be a good listener first and a small mouth.

Whenever you want to know more about a person, the trick is to ask questions that give the person room to answer away. These are called open-ended questions. Asking questions whose obvious answers are yes or no is not going to help you here. Questions that require the person to speak about them, their challenges, and their strengths are what you really need. Another way to approach this situation is to talk to the person and share stories from your own life where you have done something helpful for other people. Most of the time, you will find people telling you that they have been facing something similar in their life, and this conversation will help you a lot. For starters, it will help you to understand what this person truly needs.

One of the first mistakes that people make is that they think not everyone has triggers. But you are wrong here – everyone has them. The only difference is that some people are really good at hiding their triggers. If it is of any help, I am going to give you examples of some of the most common hot buttons that people have –

- **Fear** – The reason why I am mentioning fear at the beginning of this list is because it is the most powerful hot button of all. Two of the most common situations when fear shows itself as a hot button in a person is when they are trying to avoid pain or when they are trying to seek pleasure. But you also have to keep in mind that fear does not act in the same way for everyone. What you fear in life might not be the same for someone else and vice-versa. Fear depends on the experiences that people have in their lives. So, if you notice this hot button in the person, you have to use it to your benefit. Give them a solution that removes their fear, and this option should eliminate all doubts.

- **Anger** – The next hot button on the list is anger. Anger is something we all experience in our daily lives, and to be honest, quite frequently. But what is important here is that you have to notice how someone is reacting to this emotion and how this emotion is affecting their ability to form decisions. If there are any choices that you are looking to change, then you have to keep an eye on how anger is influencing those choices in the person. But if you want to use this hot button for your own benefits, the first thing that you should do is try and understand it.
- **Greed** – We make the mistake of thinking that only some people are capable of greed. But no, greed is present in some form in all of us. The degree of green in a person varies, and yet, it is still there. Greed is mostly about a fear that you won't get anything out of a situation and that you will be left lonely.

This gives rise to the thought that no one can take things from you when you have everything. This makes people go to great lengths just because they are looking for approval and acceptance.

Once you recognize the hot buttons of the person, it will also help you understand his/her values. Hot buttons make people angry, and this anger is rooted in the feeling that whatever they had expected didn't happen. So, their expectations have been violated. Moreover, whenever someone is in a situation where their hot buttons are triggered, they automatically become defensive. Understanding this will help you figure out the reason behind someone's behavior.

Keep an Eye on Nonverbal Communication

Nonverbal communication is often overlooked, and yet it is one of the most useful tools that you can yield to understand people around you. It will not only help you engage with a person but also relate to him/her and have more meaningful chats. A major part of nonverbal communication is about body language and we are going to talk about it indepth in Part 3 of this book, but for now, I will give you an overall idea.

Every movement made by the human body means something, and this can mean something as simple as directions of the eyes. Understanding these cues will help you understand what signals the person is trying to send through his/her gestures. You can say that nonverbal communication constitutes the subtle sound in a conversation that people often don't pay attention to. So, let us have a look at the different types of nonverbal communication that are there –

- Eye movements
- Tone of voice
- Gestures
- Body movements
- Postures
- Facial expressions

If you want to make a verbal message much clearer, then you should apply it in conjunction with these nonverbal cues. This can even be used to contradict someone's opinions. Understanding the nonverbal cues of a person is usually easier when both of you are already in a relationship or are close to each other. This, in turn, strengthens your bonds.

Another thing to be aware of here in order to avoid any misunderstandings is that different cultures have different meanings for the aspects of nonverbal communication. For example, a gesture in Thailand may mean one thing and something completely different in the United States. Similarly, many cultures do not believe in actively showing emotions through getures. They are more subtle. If you try to be too close with them too soon, they might consider it offensive. The same goes for eye contact. In the United States, you will often find people maintaining eye contact while talking because they think it means that you have an interest and also shows your trustworthiness. Whereas, the same things might be disrespectful in some Asian cultures.

Reading nonverbal cues often goes wrong when you are stressed. So, if you want to read someone's nonverbal cues, you also need to figure out how you can manage your stress. This is very important because you don't want the person to feel that they have been disrespected or misunderstood.

See the Person in a Light They Want to be Seen

Everyone has an image of themselves in their mind. No matter how many times people deny it, everyone wants to be perceived in a certain way by the society. This perception is mainly based on their beliefs. It is also termed as self-verification theory. A number of studies were done at the University of Arizona and Stanford University, where participants were chosen in a way such that there were some who had negative perceptions of themselves, and there were also those who had positive perceptions. And then, all of these participants were asked the same question – who they wanted to interact with – was it someone who had a negative impression of them or a positive impression? It was found that those participants who thought of themselves in a positive light wanted to speak with those who also thought very highly of them. At the same time, critics were preferred by those participants who had a negative perception of themselves (Dawn T. Robinson, 1992).

The most likely explanation is that people like to spend time with those who provide them feedback that is along the same lines as their perception of themselves.

Then, there have been other studies that suggest that it is much smoother when people's perceptions are along the same lines as self-perception of the person. This is because the person feels much more understood. So, if you want to examine someone and want them to open up to you, then you have to treat them in a way that they perceive themselves to be.

Tell Them a Secret

You must be wondering why I am asking you to reveal a secret to a person when it is you who is trying to understand him/her. Well, this is called self-disclosure, and it is very effective when it comes to examining others. It is one of the best techniques for building a relationship with people. Once you have confided in a person with your secret, it will automatically build a bond. Now, you don't have to tell him/her a true secret – you can make something up just for the time being. You simply have to show that you consider them trustworthy, and then you will find them opening up to you too.

There are several components to being trustworthy. It is not only about keeping a secret but also about loyalty, trust, and, more importantly, dependability. All of these factors are extremely important in relationships. You have to make the person feel that you are the right person to open up to.

So, these were some of the simplest psychological tricks that you can apply to examine others, make them open up to you, and also understand their hidden motives. This brings us to our next topic – Emotional Intelligence or EQ that you will find in the next part of this book.

Part 3 – Emotional Intelligence

In this part of the book, I am going to tell you everything there is to know about Emotional Intelligence or which is commonly referred to as EI. Many people are confused about whether emotional intelligence is something that people are born with, or is it learned? Well, I'd say it's both. There are some people who truly are born with this gift, but for those who aren't, don't worry because it can most certainly be learned. All you have to do is follow the techniques and give your best effort to understand others by putting yourself in their shoes.

When you become emotionally intelligent, you become more emotionally self-aware, and this will benefit you in all spheres of your life. In fact, in today's world, if a comparison between EI and IQ is done, you will find that EI has become way more important. In Chapter, you will get a basic introduction of what EI means, and then we will move on to the more advanced topics. By the end of this book, you will become an expert at negotiating in conflicting situations, relating to others no matter how difficult the situation is, and also improve your teamwork skills. In short, if you want a balanced life, emotional intelligence is a skill that you should master.

Chapter 1: What is Emotional Intelligence?

'Intelligence' is a term with which almost all people are very much familiar. Besides being familiar, it is equally important as it is a person's ability to learn something, applying the knowledge, and trying to solve problems. Emotional intelligence (EI) or being emotionally intelligent is an entirely new concept for a large number of people. This concept, as well as the term, was popularized in the 1990s by efficient researchers. You might be quite surprised to know that emotional intelligence is different from general intelligence. For those of you who are willing to gather more information about emotional intelligence have certainly clicked in the right place. Here you will get to know a lot of facts about this essential concept.

A true fact is that all people do not possess the capability of understanding and valuing the feelings and emotions of their own selves as well as others. But, many are also available who have this essential quality. Emotional intelligence is all about an individual's ability to identify or understanding and managing his or her own emotions. A lot of renowned psychologists state that emotional intelligence is one's ability to utilize the emotions by applying them to certain tasks like thinking, problem-solving, etc.

The most interesting fact is that a person who possesses this particular characteristic also bears an additional ability to understand other people's emotions. If you are the bearer of this special feature, then you will be able to influence both behavior and emotions of others. People with emotional intelligence (EI) may become extremely successful in their lives as well as in careers just because of such extra-ordinary understanding. Being aware emotionally is very much important in every single part of a person's life. If you are extremely warm-hearted, generous, polite, and patient, then your relationships will also be stronger than others. Various authentic studies reveal that 58% of the job performance of a person is directly or indirectly dependent on emotional intelligence. People who have high emotional intelligence levels earn, on average, $29,000 more money each year than those who have a low level of EI.

A maximum number of individual fails to realize whether he or she is emotionally intelligent or not. Thus, a question might arise in your mind that what are the ways to identify an emotionally intelligent person. Have a look at some of the examples for recognizing someone having emotional intelligence.

Examples of Emotional Intelligence

Here are some of the signs that indicate people having EI or emotional intelligence:

- Such people are an outstanding problem solver
- Never fail to ask straight-forward and open-minded questions
- Excellent listeners
- Does not blame others or make excuses while accepting constructive criticism
- Possess the ability to ignore as well as forgetting bad moments
- Considered as a sensitive and sympathetic person by other people
- Such people are never scared of saying 'NO'
- Do not have a fear of apologizing after admitting mistakes
- Understand the reason behind any action as well as the behavior of other people
- Possess the ability to calm down as well as cheering up another person

Besides all these examples, some signs are also available that might help you to realize that a person lacks emotional intelligence. A person who does not have this special trait may exhibit some of the below-mentioned signs.

- Holds grudges for a long time period
- Gets a feeling that he or she is misunderstood by others
- Has trouble in taking charges or responsibilities
- Unable to understand the emotion of the opposite person
- Does not have the ability to handle any feedback in the proper and positive manner
- Has the habit of getting offended very easily
- Has great difficulty in maintaining any sort of relationship, be it personal or professional
- Becomes judgemental in almost all situations
- Unable to move on by forgetting about past mistakes

Importance of Emotional Intelligence

Some of the reasons why emotional intelligence is important are as follows –

- ***Being mentally well*** – EI or emotional intelligence has a great effect on how you will deal with your life and also your attitude towards everything. Emotional intelligence is also helpful in avoiding frequent mood swings, depression, etc. It even has the power to ease a person's anxiety. A high EI level may provide you a positive attitude as well as a confident outlook on your life.
- ***Relationships*** – If you are able to manage or control your own emotions well, then you will be able to communicate or express your feelings effectively and constructively. A stronger and successful relationship can be maintained if you have the ability to relate to the feelings, responses, and needs of those individuals for whom you care.
- ***Physical health*** – A person who is aware of the ways of handling stress will surely be able to maintain good emotional as well as general health. Thus, it is necessary to take care of your body as it affects your well-being immensely.
- ***Conflict resolution*** – An individual will find it easier to resolve or avoid any sort of conflict if he or she possesses the ability to recognize other people's emotions as well as

understanding their viewpoint. As emotionally intelligent individuals are good at understanding the needs and desires of almost all other people, so they can settle down with any disputes and adjust accordingly.

- ***Success*** – For being successful in almost all sectors of life, a person's hesitation level must be very low, along with enhanced self-belief and a high level of concentration. All such features are available in an emotionally aware person. Emotional intelligence is highly important as it helps a person in possessing a strong and flexible outlook towards life. It even assists an individual to overcome setbacks very easily.

Thus, to be successful in your life as well as career, developing emotional intelligence has become very much essential. Your overall success will entirely depend on your ability to identify the signals given by other people and responding appropriately.

Chapter 2: How to Increase Your Emotional Intelligence Skills?

In the professional world, emotional intelligence or EQ continues to gain popularity. Emotional intelligence is not a trend. In an evolving workplace, EQ continues to gain importance among co-workers and peers, and several companies have gathered statistical evidence that EQ undoubtedly affects the bottom line. Companies having employees with higher levels of EQ have found drastic improvement in total productivity and sales.

You can build your emotional intelligence at any time. However, you have to remember that just learning about EQ is different from applying that knowledge to your daily life. Sometimes you fail to do something even though you know that you should do it. It especially occurs when you get overwhelmed by stress, and this can outweigh even your best intentions. In order to stay emotionally aware and permanently change your behaviors so that they can withstand any stress, you have to learn how to overcome pressures in your relationships and the present moment.

Some of the main skills needed to build your emotional intelligence and boost your ability to connect with other people and manage your feelings are:

1. Relationship management
2. Social awareness
3. Self-awareness
4. Self-management
5. Self-motivation

Relationship Management

The process of working properly with others starts with your ability to identify and analyze what other people are going through and with your emotional awareness. You can effectively develop other social and emotional skills once your emotional awareness comes into play. Through this, you can make your relationships more fulfilling, fruitful, and effective.

- **Learn to see any differences as a chance to get closer to others** – In any human relationship, disagreements and conflicts are inevitable. Two different individuals can never have all the same expectations, opinions, and requirements all the time. However, that is not necessarily a bad thing. The trust between two people can actually get even stronger when the conflict is resolved in a healthy and constructive way. When the conflicts and disagreements are not seen as something punishing and threatening, it can develop safety, creativity, and freedom in relationships.

- **Use play and humor to alleviate stress** – Play, laughter, and humor are considered to be the natural antidotes to stress. They help you in keeping things in perspective by decreasing your burdens. Laughter can make you more empathic by sharpening your mind, calming you down, reducing your stress levels, and balancing your nervous system.

- **Stay aware of how you are using non-verbal communication** – It is not possible to prevent yourself from sending non-verbal messages to other people regarding what you are feeling and thinking. Your emotions are wordlessly conveyed through the several muscles present in your face, particularly those surrounding your forehead, mouth, nose, and eyes. These muscles also help you read someone else's emotional intent. The region of your brain that is in control of these non-verbal methods of communication is always active, and even if you try to ignore those messages, other people won't. You can improve your relationships immensely by identifying the non-verbal messages that you keep sending to other people.

The whole idea behind developing emotional intelligence should be to create and maintain healthier relationships in your life. Any healthy relationship, whether it's friendships, familial relationships, or romantic relationships, start with respecting and identifying each other's emotional requirements. You have to connect with others and empathize with them. You can do this by listening to other people and sharing your honest self with them.

When you are empathizing with an individual, it doesn't really mean that you have to completely understand them. Instead, it means that you should learn to accept their real selves, even if you don't understand them. You have to understand that you need to treat them as an end in themselves and value their existence instead of as a means for something else. You accept their suffering as your own suffering – as your collective suffering.

With the help of relationships, you can get yourself out of your head and enter the real world. They help you realize that you are a part of something much more complex and bigger than just yourself.

Social Awareness

With the help of social awareness, you can identify and understand the many non-verbal cues that other people are continuously using to communicate with you. These cues help you know what's truly important to them, how their emotional state is continuing to change, and how they are feeling. When groups of people start conveying their feelings through such non-verbal cues, you can read and interpret the share emotional experiences and power dynamics of the group. All in all, you become socially comfortable and empathetic.

You need to understand the importance of mindfulness in order to create social awareness. Mindfulness is a friend of social and emotional awareness. This is because, when you are zoning out on your phone or thinking about other stuff, you probably won't be able to detect subtle non-verbal cues. You are required to be present at the moment to be socially aware and detect such cues. Even though several people are proud of the fact that they can multitask, this also suggests that they will not be able to detect the subtle shifts in emotions that take place in the people around them that will help them understand them completely.

- You have to pay attention to your personal emotional changes in order to follow the

flow of someone else's emotional responses. It's a give-and-take process.
- By keeping your entire focus on the interaction you're having and setting all other thoughts aside, you can increase your social goals even further.
- Your own self-awareness is not diminished when you pay attention to others. You can actually get an insight into your own beliefs, values, and emotional state when you invest your effort and time to really pay attention to someone else. For instance, when you listen to others expressing their views, you might feel or some other emotion. Through this, you can also learn something important about yourself.

Self-Awareness

One of the most important steps to building emotional intelligence is managing stress. According to the science of attachment, your present emotional experience is most possibly a reflection of the experiences of your early life. Your ability to control core feelings like joy, fear, sadness, and anger generally depends on the consistency and the quality of the emotional experiences you had in your early life. For example, if, as an infant, your primary caretaker understood and valued your feelings, it is possible that in adult life, your emotions have become valuable assets. However, if your experiences as an infant were painful, threatening, or baffling, it's possible that you have distanced yourself from certain emotions because of that.

The process of self-awareness consists of understanding yourself and your behavior on three different stages: what you're doing, how you're feeling about the task, and trying to identify the things that you don't know about yourself.

- **Knowing what you are feeling** – It might freak you out at first when you focus on how you are feeling. You might come to realize that you have often appeared too angry or too sad to several people in your life. You might come to realize that you are under a lot of stress and anxiety, and you use your phone as a method to continuously distract and numb yourself from that feeling of anxiety. At this point, it is essential that you don't judge the feelings that are rising. If you ignore it, it might just get worse.
- **Knowing what you are doing** – You might think that knowing what you are doing at a particular moment is very straightforward and simple. However, this is not the case in

the twenty-first century. Half of the time, people are on auto-pilot and don't really know what they are doing. Eliminating some distractions from your life every now and then and engaging in the real world can help you gain self-awareness. Even though it might seem scary, searching for spaces of solitude and silence are essential for your mental health. Some forms of distraction include using your phone, cross-stitching, video games, alcohol, drugs, TV, work, etc. Try to get away from such distractions by scheduling some time in your day. Try commuting in the morning without any podcast or music. Just think about what you are feeling at the moment. Keep ten minutes aside in your schedule and try meditation.

- People often use such distractions to avoid facing several uncomfortable feelings and situations. Therefore, try to concentrate on how you are feeling without those distractions.
- **Knowing your own emotions** – Once you start noticing all the uncomfortable emotions you are feeling, you will start getting a sense of where your own crazy thoughts reside. By being aware of those emotions, you can act against them.

The key to understanding how your emotions affect your actions and thoughts lies in being able to connect with your emotions. Ask yourself the following questions:

- Do you concentrate on your emotions? Do you consider your emotions while making your decisions?
- Do you feel intense emotions that are strong enough to seize both your as well as someone else's attention?
- Do you experience individual emotions and feelings like joy, fear, sadness, and anger; each of such emotions is conveyed by subtle facial expressions?
- Do you experience physical sensations in your chest, throat, or stomach, along with your emotions?
- Do you feel your emotions in a flow and experience one emotion after another as they keep changing from one moment to another?

If any of these experiences seem unfamiliar to you, it means you might have turned off or turned down your emotions. To become emotionally healthy and build your emotional intelligence, you need to reconnect with your core emotions and accept them to get comfortable with yourself.

Self-Management

You should be able to utilize your emotions and take constructive decisions regarding your behavior to be able to engage your EQ. you can lose command over your feelings and your ability to act appropriately and thoughtfully if you get extremely stressed. Think back to the time when you were overcome by stress. Was it easy to make a rational decision or think clearly? It probably wasn't. When you are under acute stress, your ability to correctly and precisely assess someone's emotions and think clearly gets compromised.

Emotions are extremely important bits of information that can tell you about yourself and other people. However, when you are in stress, it can take you out of your comfort zone. When this happens, you get overwhelmed and lose control of yourself. By developing emotional intelligence, you can develop the ability to stay emotionally present and manage your stress levels. You can teach yourself how to receive troubling information without allowing it to override your self-control and your thoughts. You will then be able to make decisions that help you adapt to changing circumstances, follow through on commitments, take the initiative, control your emotions in a healthy manner, and control impulsive behaviors and feelings.

Self-Motivation

Have you ever lost yourself completely while doing something? For instance, you begin an activity and get completely engrossed in it, and then when you finally snap out of the self-induced hypnotic state that you have put yourself in, you notice that 3 hours have gone by although it felt like only fifteen minutes. You might feel a combination of fascination, slightly frustrated intrigue, and small bursts of dopamine at these moments. This feeling can further motivate you to continue doing something you love.

This feeling is often known as the "Do Something Principle," and it is one of the simplest and most magical hacks there is. It conveys that doing an activity or performing an action is not only the effect of motivation, but it can also be the cause of motivation.

Tips to Improve Your Emotional Intelligence Skills

Here are some tips through which you can increase your emotional awareness skills:

- **Be sociable and approachable –** Emotionally intelligent people tend to appear more approachable. They give off a positive vibe through their smile and presence. They are able to make use of proper social skills on the basis of their relationship with the people around them. Irrespective of whether the communication is verbal or non-verbal, they can communicate clearly and have great interpersonal skills.

- **Use leadership skills** – People with emotional intelligence skills have very good leadership skills. They set an example for other people to follow as they have high standards. They have excellent problem-solving and decision-making skills, and they tend to take the initiative. This lets them give a better and more productive level of performance, not only at work but also in life.
- **Empathize with others** – People with emotional intelligence know how to empathize. They have realized the fact that empathy is a trait that doesn't show your weakness, and rather it shows your emotional strength. With the help of empathy, they can relate to other people on a basic human level. It helps them open a way for mutual understanding and respect between different individuals with separate situations and opinions.
- **Take critique well –** An important aspect of improving your EQ skills is to be able to

receive any critique in a calm and composed manner instead of getting defensive or offended. People with high EQ are able to take some time and understand where that critique is coming from, how it's affecting their performance and that of others, and how they can act to sort out any issue.

- **Try to maintain a positive attitude** – The power of your attitude should never be underestimated. A negative attitude can easily infect another person if they let it. People with a high EQ can guard their moods in accordance to the moods of the people around them. They know what they should do so that they have an optimistic outlook and thereby a good day. This could include saving some positive sayings in their computer or sticking them at their desk, engaging in meditation or prayer in the daytime, or having an amazing breakfast or lunch.

- **Don't forget to breathe** – Life tends to throw different situations your way. And a majority of you have experienced the stress of some kind in your daily life. Don't forget to breathe when this happens. It will help you to deal with your emotions and avoid any outbursts. Try to take a pause and make a drink or go outside to get some fresh air or splash some fresh water on your face. Do something that will give yourself some time to understand what's happening so that you can keep your cool and decide how you should respond.

- **Don't complain** – Complaining generally conveys two things – that there's no solution to our problems, and that we are the victims. A person with high EQ will rarely feel victimized or feel that a solution is out of their reach. Therefore, try to think constructively and resolve the problem in private instead of searching for something or someone to put the blame on.

Chapter 3: What is Speed Reading and How Can You Do It?

Do you face situations where work keeps piling in front of you, and you have very little time to finish them? Well, I guess all of us have faced such a situation at least once in our lives. The clock keeps ticking, and you have a ton of paperwork to read through. You do not have the option of asking for an extension. You cannot afford to make mistakes; otherwise, you will look careless. And on top of everything, you start panicking. So, if you want to grasp all the information from those materials you have without having to go through each and every word, then what you need to learn is speed reading.

If speed reading is a concept that is new to you, don't worry because, in this chapter, I am not only going to explain what it means, but I am also going to show you the different techniques that you can use to learn speed reading. We shall also go over some of the advantages and disadvantages of this process, and you will have a clear idea of when you can use it and when you can't.

Before moving any further, let me give you a definition of speed reading. It is a process of reading where you kind of absorb the sentences or phrases on a single page at the same time, and you don't have to go through each and every word like in traditional reading. Every day human beings are now processing more and more information, and this includes stuff on social media, at work, magazines, books, and reading emails. But the time at our hands is still the same, and so, it is quite natural that people feel stressed. Everyone is under this immense pressure of understanding everything as fast as they can so that they can make the necessary decisions. Everyone wants to stay in the loop.

Usually, 250 words per minute is the average rate of reading in most people, but there are some who are different because they can read quickly naturally. If these people were to learn speed reading, their speed of reading will become even better.

When Should You Speed Read?

Now, you already know that the main aim of speed reading is to help you decrease the time in which you complete reading one page. But is speed reading appropriate in every situation, or is there any particular situation where you shouldn't be using it?

You need to understand that for speed reading to be effective, you have to strike a balance between comprehension and pace. There have been various studies in this field that have shown that the amount of information taken in often gets reduced with the faster you read. This applies even more, when it involves too many details.

So, let us say that you have to go through some document that is highly technical and has a lot of details in it that you have to understand in order to process it or summarize it. Will speed reading be the answer to your question in that situation? No. No matter how less the time at your hands is, you should not speed read such documents which involve a lot of technicalities. At the same time, if you are reading something that is of unfamiliar genre or is something new, you should consider slowing down. The same theory applies to a teacher when he/she is going through a material with the aim of teaching someone else. But speed reading can definitely be a handy approach when you simply have to understand the conclusion of some material that is simple and mainstream, or you have to figure out the basic arguments.

Speed reading can also be used when you are re-reading something. In a study conducted in 1934, it was found that comprehension skills can really improve when someone uses speed reading techniques while going through the prose second time around (McClusky, 1934).

If we are speaking generally, reading has to be done at a slower pace when you are trying to memorize the material. The average reading speed in such a situation is 100 words per minute. For learning, the normal rate of reading is 100-200 words per minute, and when it comes to comprehension, it is 200-400 words per minute. As far as speed reading is concerned, the average reading speed is 400-700 words per minute. But if someone reads at a rate of 500-600 words per minute or more, then it simply means that they are compromising comprehension. But I must say that these rates vary from one person to the other.

Techniques For Speed Reading

In this section, we are going to learn some of the techniques for speed reading that everyone should give a try.

Let Go of the Inner Monologue

First, let me explain what the inner monologue is. The term subvocalization is also used to define it. Most readers have this problem. But what does it mean? It is the tendency to speak the words in the mind while reading. This trait is a barrier in speed reading.

When you read, you will often find your own voice reading along with you inside your head. This is a habit that is inculcated in us since our childhood. Every teacher has said this – repeat the words silently in your mind while you read. A young reader picks up this habit, and this is what gives birth to the inner monologue.

In the initial days, children are taught to read out loud and slowly, when they become an expert at that, they are asked to repeat the words in their minds. This is where the origin of this habit lies, and kids carry this habit into adulthood as well. The habit will not affect you negatively until and unless you want to increase your reading speed.

When it comes to learning speed reading,

overcoming the inner monologue is the first hurdle that you have to cross.

It has been found that the average talking speed and reading speed of a person are more or less the same. This is because of subvocalization – the reading speed is limited by the speed at which a person can talk because they are repeating each word in their head. So, if you want to forget the inner monologue and read without it, then you have to tell yourself that the inner monologue serves no purpose. It was necessary at a young age, but now you are an adult, and it is not necessary for you to carry on with it.

If you are still finding it hard to overcome this habit, you can start reading with music on and putting on your earphones. Or, you can also try chewing gum while reading. You will not focus on subvocalization where there is something else going on in the background. Then, you will realize that you can still process the words by just looking at them.

Learn Word Chunking

This step is also very much related to getting over the inner monologue. As you might have understood from the term, word chunking is a concept where you learn to read more than one word at the same time by clubbing them together. It is also one of the most effective methods that will increase your reading speed. Yes, it is true that since childhood, we are taught to read a passage word by word, but even then, we can read by clubbing words together. This process becomes much easier when you put your peripheral vision into action. We will talk more about that in the next point.

But in order to take the first step, you must practice reading at least three words together and then continue reading the passage in the same manner. Note down the time in which you finished reading a particular text. You will notice that even when you clubbed those words together, you were able to make meaning out of the prose, but the only difference is that you did not spend too much time reading it.

Once you master this, it is time that you take the next step. Take a page and draw two vertical lines on it that will divide the text into three sections. Now, start reading, but you have to keep in mind that whatever is in one section, you will read it as one chunk of word. Now, finish reading the page and note down the time. You will see that you have finished way before that your previous time.

Stop Rereading the Same Words

I am going to talk about how you can use peripheral vision to speed read, but before that, you also have to eliminate the habit of rereading words on the same page. Most people jump between sentences – they reread the sentence that they went over just now. This is also one of the barriers to practicing speed reading.

If you think about it, you might notice that you have this habit too, but you didn't realize it until today. The fact that most people are not even awar that they do this makes this an even trickier thing to overcome. But let me give you an inside tip as to how you can overcome this habit – use your finger while reading. I know it sounds childish but it works. Your finger will help you track the words as you keep reading and prevents you from going back to the previous sentence.

Learn to Use Your Peripheral Vision

Now, we come to the step that you all have been waiting for – how to use your peripheral vision to increase your reading speed? It is not the final step in this list, but it is definitely one of the most important ones.

In the beginning, you learned the concept of word chunking. Here, instead of forming small chunks, you will read one line at a time, but how? Start by looking at the center of the sentence, and then with the help of peripheral vision, you will read the sides. You have to keep reading the whole page in the same manner until you reach the end. You will find that the time taken was much less, and yet you understood everything you read.

Always Keep a Timer

If you want to learn speed reading, then having a timer with you at all times is very essential. The timer will help you understand how much you have improved since the beginning. Keep track of the time you took reading a single page using various methods. You can also track your improvement by setting the timer for a particular span of time and then seeing how many pages you were able to ready by the time the timer went off.

Keeping track of time from the beginning will help you visualize your improvement, and this will also keep you motivated to do better. Your aim should be to beat your previous record, and in this way, you can strive to do better every time.

Improve Your Vocabulary

People often overlook the fact that your vocabulary has to be good if you want to make the best out of speed reading. Think about it this way – what good is speed reading if most of the words you come across in the passage are new to you? Do you skip those words just because you have to finish reading on time? Or, do you try to figure out the meaning by analyzing the context in which it is used? Or, are you someone who sits with a dictionary in hand so that you can look up any new word that you come accorss? No matter which of the options resonates with you, all of them will hamper your reading speed. The only way out is to know the meaning of more and more words, and for that, you have to work on your vocabulary. You can read faster when you know the meaning of more words.

Apply the Tactics That You Have Read

Lastly, I want to say that you have to start applying these tactics in real life to see how much you have learned and whether it is helping you or not. Learning the tactics is really good, but it won't be of any help if you don't apply them. So, start today!

Tips to Read Faster

You have already gone through the basics of speed reading, and now, I am going to give you some final tips on how you can improve your reading speed.

- **Steer clear of distractions** – The first thing that you should do is keep all the distractions at bay. Your reading environment should be peaceful and minimize the distractions as much as you can. This will enable you to maintain your focus entirely on the passage that you are reading. There must be no noise.

- **Start easy** – I have seen many people who start speed reading with difficult passages. But that's not what you should do. Start with something easy and relevant because that will help you master the tactics. It can be a simple article you got online or an uncomplicated novel. This will also help you understand which technique of speed reading is helping you the most. You also have to understand what you are reading, so analyze how much you were able to memorize or understand. Also, sit with a timer so that you can measure your time every time you read.
- **Maintain a positive attitude** – Your attitude is what determines your success. If you are negative right from the start that you won't be able to master speed reading, then you are not going to achieve success. But if you practice self-affirmations and believe that you are doing better than yesterday, you will be able to see the improvements for yourself.
- **Read more** – Lastly, keep reading more books, and you have to understand just like

everything else you learn, reading is a skill. It won't improve overnight. You have to give it time. You will become better if you read more. Set goals because they will help you to look forward to something. You can set weekly goals if daily goals are something that seems too intimidating for you. You can also have yearly goals of reading a particular number of books. But at the same time, you have to remember that reading is not a race. When you set goals and plan your reading, it simply helps you to block time for it on your calendar and makes sure you read every day.

So, these were some of the tips that you should remember. All in all, remember to reverse all the bad habits that you have, starting from subvocalizing to rereading sentences because these are going to be the real barriers in your path. Once you figure out a way to manage these problems, the rest of the process is much easier. In case you feel overwhelmed, try to handle one thing at a time, and in a few days, you will become an expert speed-reader.

Chapter 4: 7 Body Language Examples and What Do They Show?

Whenever we are with someone, we are displaying some kind of body language either knowingly or unknowingly, and every move has a meaning. In this chapter, you will learn everything there is to know about body language and how you can use them to improve your communication skills. For this, I am going to give you examples of different types of body language and then explain to you what they really mean.

If I have to frame in simple words, body language is that part of communication which is unspoken, and yet it speaks volumes about the person. It reveals a lot about a person's motives and intentions. It includes facial expressions, gestures, and posture. If you learn to read the different body language people display and what they mean, you will surely be able to use this knowledge to your advantage. You will also become more aware of what others are actually trying to say and whether they have any hidden motives. This entire process of understanding nonverbal communication is quite fun and powerful at the same time.

Body language can be of two types – positive body language and negative body language. The former will help you use it to your benefit to land clients, enhance a romantic bond, or even win an argument. On the other hand, negative body language is what affects you negatively and offends people. Then there are microexpressions too – these are expressions which occur for a very brief moment of time, maybe 1/25th of a second. Microexpressions usually show themselves when a person is trying their best to hide an intense emotion.

So, here are some common examples that everyone should know.

Smile

The first example that we are going to discuss is a smile. A smile might have multiple meanings attached to it. In order to decipher it's meaning, you have to know about the different types of smiles that are there. Smile is one of the fundamental things about facial expression in humans. You can even call it a reflex. But did you know that smile is controlled by a total of 17 pairs of muscles? There are shy smiles, and there are happy smiles. The Duchenne smile is quite characteristic – it is the one where a person smiles so wide that the corners of the mouth are stretched sideways, and there is the formation of crow's feet at the corner of the eyes. The Duchenne smile is often considered to be one of the most genuine smiles in the world. And then there is the fake smile, which is when the person does not have any emotion in the smile and is simply showing his/her teeth.

I don't know whether you have heard of the term 'smiling eyes' or not, but it is an expression that is used to refer to people who have the ability to communicate their smile directly through eye contact. If you notice a Duchenne smile in someone, you should understand that they are friendly and approachable.

Arms Crossed on Chest

This is another very common body language that you must understand. The folden arms position is one that is often interpreted to be a form of disagreement. Understanding this body language is important if you want the person to understand your message clearly. This body language also means that you will need a really good ice-breaker for the person to become approachable and receptive to what you have to say.

It is quite reasonable to think that the person disagrees with you when you see them crossing their arms on the chest just after you said something. In that case, you have to understand that pursuing the conversation along the same lines is going to be of no use. Your aim should be to make the person more receptive. As long as the person remains in that position, they are very likely to disagree with whatever you are going to say.

So, here is a tip – you should give them something, for example, a pen or some refreshment that would force them to break their position. This is how you make them more open to what you are going to say. Another very common tactic that helps is asking someone to look at a presentation or anything else that requires them to lean down.

Another thing that you should look out for is whether the person has clenched fists along with crossed arms. If yes, then this means that the person is both defensive and hostile. You can attack a physical or verbal attack if this position is accompanied by clenched teeth. If you cannot seem to figure out the reason, you need to move forward with a conciliatory approach.

Eyebrows

Next, let's move back to another aspect of facial expressions – the eyebrows. The first thing that all of us do whenever we meet someone is we greet them. Raising one's eyebrows is one of the most common gestures people make when they meet someone. But what does that mean? It simply means that the person is acknowledging you, and sometimes, it also means that they think you both have things in common. When someone raises their eyebrows while greeting, the other person automatically feels that they are obliged to do so too.

In fact, if you don't believe me, try this tactic on someone who is a stranger to you. If you greet them and raise your eyebrows, they will do the same. This is because that single expression makes them feel that they might know you in some way. So, when can you use this tactic to your benefit? If you are going to a business meeting where you have to meet a client and impress them, then I'd say that you should raise your eyebrows during the greeting. It also helps when you are going for a negotiation. This simple 'eyebrow flash' might not seem like a big deal now, but trust me when I say this, it can really set things off on the right foot for you.

The Head

In this section, we are going to discuss some of the body language signals that you get from the head. If you think about it, you will realize that none of us keeps our heads in the same position or still for a long period of time. Everyone always tries to look here and there. You might even have the habit of tilting your head to one side when you are listening to something or someone. But what is interesting is that you can understand the stress levels of a person by simply keeping an eye on the movement of their head. You can identify a sign of submission if you see that the person has bowed down their head.

But sometimes, bowing down the head also means that the person is intimidated or is shy. Also, at times, when the person is bowing their head down, they might be expecting you to disagree with them or jump into a conflict. But whatever the reason is, you can say that the person is either meek, vulnerable or stressed when they are bowing their heads down.

However, there are some situations where this prediction is not going to work. Do you know why? It is because, in those moments, the person is bowing down just because he/she is bored. This happens in those long meetings or presentations that we all hate.

Now, let us move to some positive notes. You can say that the person is confident if they hold their head up high. This also shows how relaxed they are and that they are pretty sure about what they are doing. They are highly focused on what is happening, and there is no chance of conflict right now.

Lips & Eyes

These two features make up about 80% of the total number of facial expressions that human beings have. If you think about it, you will realize that your eyes become sad when you are sad, and your lips also stoop down. On the contrary, when you are happy, there is a sparkle in your eyes. And all of these expressions are quite automatic and happen on their own. A person is often deemed to be confident when they look at you directly in the eyes while talking. But yes, even this should not go to an extreme extent; otherwise, it can become comfortable.

Similarly, a person can be deemed to be worried or defensive if they try to avoid eye contact and look here and there during the conversation. Another trick that you should know is when the eyes are downcast. If you notice this, then you should understand that the person is not really paying any attention to what you are saying. Eye signals are extremely important when you are trying to negotiate a deal in your favor or when you are in a job interview. So, if you are talking to someone and you want to impress them, look into their eyes but don't creep them out.

Neck

There is a natural human tendency to touch the neck whenever a person feels stressed. People specifically touch the area of the throat because psychology says that humans want to somehow protect it whenever they are in a situation that is defensive. In men, you will find that they are touching their tie from time to time or fiddling with it. Some men even stroke their beard or the chin area. In the case of women, however, the area just beneath Adam's apple is where they touch. And, there are also some women who might fiddle with their ring or pendant.

Crossing the Legs

The way in which you sit also says a lot about the person you are or what you are thinking. When someone crosses their legs towards the ankle, then it is usually predicted that they are trying to hide something. A person is usually uncomfortable in the place when they cross their legs at the knees, and the position of the knees is turned away from the person they are talking to. If you don't want people to understand your emotional state from how you sit, the best thing you can do is put your legs on the ground firmly.

Conclusion

Thank you for making it through to the end of *Book Title*, let's hope it was informative and able to provide you with all of the tools you need to achieve your goals, whatever they may be.

I agree that there is no end to how much you can learn about the psychology of people. But by now, I expect that you have understood to distinguish the manipulators from the good people and also how you can use the mind control techniques to your benefit. The most important thing that you need to understand is that your life is in your hands. If you allow people to prey on you, then they are going to walk all over you. But if you sharpen your emotional intelligence skills and be more self-aware, you can prevent all of that and stay one step ahead at all times.

I have tried to clarify all those concepts, which are often considered taboo, like, hypnosis. There are so many myths that people are not even aware of the real truth. I have tried to break it down to you in the simplest way possible. Emotional intelligence is something that needs no special introduction, and I have tried to cover most of the topics in the most concise way possible. I hope you were able to learn a thing or two from this book and apply the tactics in your life. The strategies mentioned here are quite effective, and they will not only help you get a better grip on your life, but you will also learn how to adapt to any social setting.

Finally, if you found this book useful in any way, a review on Amazon is always appreciated!

Resources

Andrea K. Webb, D. J. (2009). Eye Movements and Pupil Size Reveal Deception in Computer Administered Questionnaires. *Foundations of Augmented Cognition. Neuroergonomics and Operational Neuroscience*, 553-562.

Dawn T. Robinson, L. S.-L. (1992). Selective Interaction as a Strategy for Identity Maintenance: An Affect Control Model. *Social Psychology Quarterly, 55*(1), 12.

Eckhard H. Hess, A. L. (1965). Pupil response of hetero- and homosexual males to pictures of men and women: A pilot study. *Journal of Abnormal Psychology, 70*(3), 165-168.

Lewis R. Goldberg. (1992). The development of markers for the Big-Five factor structure. *Psychological Assessment, 4*(1), 26-42.

McClusky, H. Y. (1934). An experiment on the influence of preliminary skimming on reading. *Journal of Educational Psychology, 25*(7), 521-529.

Stanley Milgram, L. B. (1969). Note on the drawing power of crowds of different size. *Journal of Personality and Social Psychology, 13*(2), 79-82.